TURNING
POINTS

TURNING POINTS

More Lessons Learned on Leadership, Education, and Personal Growth

*"Easy to read and full of practical advice, this book
will impact how you approach work and life."*
—JIMMY CASAS, author of Culturize

JARED R. SMITH, PhD

To my grandma,
Theresa Margaret Schiffer

Thanks for always being my biggest supporter
and for keeping me in your ongoing thoughts and prayers.

Love,
Jared aka "Number One"

TABLE OF CONTENTS

INTRODUCTION

"It's not whether you get knocked down;
it's whether you get back up." [1]

—FROM *Run to Daylight*
BY VINCE LOMBARDI

■ ■ ■

"You're just not ready."

Those were the superintendent's words when he informed me that I did not get the middle school principal job.

This was not the first of these calls. I had now interviewed for three principal jobs within the Waterloo Community School District, and all three times I was told, *"You're not good enough."*

The year was 2014 and I was in my sixth year as an assistant principal. Whereas my administrative peers were getting opportunities to lead buildings . . . all I was getting were rejection phone calls.

Upon hanging up the phone, I sat motionless in my tiny corner office. Sick to my stomach and unable to focus, I said, *"Screw it"* and left work early without telling anyone.

When I got into my black 2005 Yukon, I grabbed my case of burned CDs and pulled out a disk with the word "Revenge" written in black Sharpie. During my drive to the gym across town, I blasted Linkin Park's "Numb"; Eminem's "'Till I Collapse" (NSFW); and Tupac's "Hit 'Em Up" (*definitely* NSFW).

During my workout, several thoughts went through my head:

What am I doing wrong in my interviews?
I know I'm better than whoever they picked!
Does someone in the district office hate me?
My friends and family will think I'm a loser!
Do I have what it takes to be a principal?

The next few days were more of the same. Feelings of embarrassment, anger, and inadequacy circled my mind like a washing machine on spin cycle. These constant negative thoughts made it difficult to eat and impossible to sleep.

Eventually I reached a point of extreme mental fatigue which forced me to stay home from work. Staring blankly at the ceiling while lying in bed, I realized I was at a crossroads:

Do I quit education and transition to another profession?
Or, do I continue to grind and trust that I'll get my chance?

I grabbed my laptop and searched several job sites looking for opportunities outside of education. *"Website developer—I could do that,"* I thought to myself. *"Ooohhh—personal training sounds fun!"*

After going down the job-search rabbit hole, I switched my attention to YouTube. Searching for inspiration, I typed, *"How to move up at work"* into the navigation bar.

Three pages worth of results later, I stumbled upon an interview with comedian Steve Martin. In this particular video clip, Martin was asked to give advice on how to be successful. The following was his response:

> *When people ask me: "How do you make it in show business?" what I always tell them is not the answer they want to hear. What they want to hear is: "Here's how you get an agent . . . Here's how you write a script." But what I always say is: "Be so good they can't ignore you." If you are really good, people are going to come to you.*[2]

Little did I realize that Martin's advice—more specifically, *"Be so good they can't ignore you"*—would be the exact words needed to jump-start my stagnant professional career.

■ ■ ■

Fast forward to 2022.

On a cold, blustery day in late January I had another job interview. As is usual in school leadership, the full-day interview involved meeting with several teams of staff, parents, and community members over the course of the day.

When the process ended in the late afternoon, I grabbed my materials and headed home. For the next several hours, feelings about my performance swung like a pendulum. From *"What a great day—you nailed it!"* to *"What a stupid answer—you bombed!,"* the interview committee's looming decision consumed my thinking.

Too worried to eat dinner and too exhausted to change out of my suit, I sat at the dinner table—eyes glued to my phone.

Knowing the school board planned to make a quick decision, I pleaded for my phone to ring.

Crickets.

When 9:00pm passed without a call, my optimism waned, *"They wouldn't call this late,"* I thought while brushing my teeth. *"They must have picked someone else."*

And by 9:30pm, I had completely given up: *"Forget those guys,"* I vented. *"They wouldn't know talent if hit them in the face!"*

But at 9:42—the exact moment I placed my phone on its charger before heading to bed—I received a phone call that would change my life:

"How would you like to be the superintendent of the Waterloo Community School District?"

When the consultant said those words, I couldn't believe my ears. Whereas I had been told I wasn't good enough to lead one school . . . I was now being asked to lead all 20 schools.

In the same exact school district.

Talk about full circle.

■ ■ ■

We all experience *turning points.*

Turning points are moments in life when significant change occurs. Turning points happen within our jobs, our families, our relationships, and ourselves. Some turning points are obvious— such as an ended marriage or a career change. Other turning points are more subtle—such as how a passing compliment (or criticism) becomes part of our self-identity.

My job requires me to regularly deliver speeches to large audiences. During these opportunities, I often discuss the turning points of my youth. Recalling both high points and low points, I explain how pivotal childhood moments impacted my life trajectory. When finished, spectators are asked to reveal their own turning points with a partner. Initially hesitant to share their ideas, soon the room is abuzz with audience members swapping life stories.

As it turns out, *turning points are universal.*

This book uses life's turning points to teach universal principles in the areas of leadership, education, and personal growth. Each chapter contains bite-sized pieces of content related to the overarching section. By meshing relatable anecdotes with research-based concepts, readers will discover practical ideas for use in their professional and personal life.

Despite its deliberate structure, there is no right way to read this book. Feel free to read from cover to cover, or bounce around and choose topics that pique your interest. Think of this book as a buffet: You can start with the salad bar and proceed to the main course . . . or you can go straight for dessert.

Given this book tackles numerous issues, there may be topics that do not pertain to your current situation. Simply skip those sections and come back when you believe the subject is more applicable.

However, understand that books change as you undergo different life experiences. As time passes, concepts initially deemed unimportant may later prove meaningful. Avoid permanently rejecting any ideas as they may deliver future value.

Finally, you will notice that *Learning Curve* is referenced throughout these pages. Although you are encouraged to check out my first book, doing so is hardly a prerequisite for reading *Turning Points*. Think of *Learning Curve* and *Turning Points* as interchangeable complements as opposed to a linear series.

■ ■ ■

John Dewey once said, *"We do not learn from experience . . . we learn from reflecting on experience."*

My hope is that you view this book as an opportunity to reflect on your own experiences. Whether you are looking for a few helpful ideas—or are searching for a complete mental makeover—realize that lifelong learning is always time well spent.

What are you waiting for?

Let's get started.

LEADERSHIP

"A brave leader is someone who says I see you. I hear you. I don't have all the answers, but I'm going to keep listening and asking questions." [1]

—FROM *Dare to Lead*
BY BRENÉ BROWN

INVESTING IN CULTURE

In *Delivering Happiness*, former Zappos CEO Tony Hsieh suggests the following:

"Once you have a culture—invest in it." [2]

Although this line is simple, it packs a powerful punch for educators.

As school leaders, we learn to do more with less. We always search for ways to build culture using methods that don't cost money. We give notes of appreciation, allow staff to leave early, organize staff potlucks, and cover classrooms.

However, there comes a point when school leaders exhaust all their "free" ideas: one can only approve so many jeans days! In these cases, leaders must dip into school finances for the purpose of *investing* in school culture.

But in a world where school purchases are increasingly scrutinized, how can leaders invest in school culture without getting slapped on the wrist by auditors?

■ ■ ■

Before we go any further, it's important to define school culture investments, as well as clarify the costs associated with these investments.

First, let's be clear that investments in school culture cannot be extravagant and must follow certain rules. Therefore, those hoping to take employees on a Royal Caribbean cruise or rent The Magic School (Party) Bus using district funds are out of luck.

Instead, we're looking at *strategic, occasional* instances when leaders provide gifts, facilitate activities, and organize gatherings that are of modest expense for the purpose of enhancing employee morale and engagement.

"You said, 'modest expense.' How much are we talking?"

When discussing costs, it's important to understand school budgets. While school funding varies by state, in Iowa an average-sized school district (approximately 2,000 students) will likely spend in excess of $20 million in general fund expenditures.

The general fund covers all of the day-to-day operations of running a school district, including employee compensation, supplies, textbooks, professional development, and special programming. The general fund also covers the "staff appreciation" purchases discussed in this chapter.

Given a $20 million budget, what would you guess is a reasonable percentage to invest in school culture? Five percent? Three percent? One Percent?

While those numbers sound reasonable, they are likely far too much money to spend on these types of purchases. Believe it

or not, spending *one-tenth of a percent* of the general fund budget—roughly $20,000—should be all you need to provide staff
with meaningful perks throughout the year.

"Wow," you may be thinking. *"That's such a small percentage!"*

That's exactly my point! School leaders across the country run
multimillion-dollar budgets. Yet, when asked to use school
funds to buy coffee for the teacher's lounge they say, *"I don't
think that's in the budget."*

■ ■ ■

Curious what could be done with $20,000? Below are 7
ideas used in my former school district of roughly 250 staff
members:

All-Staff Celebrations ($10,000): We host four all-staff celebra-
tions throughout the year. During these quarterly get-togethers,
we serve food, recognize employees, play games, and give away
prizes. Our staff relishes this opportunity to connect with colleagues in a laid-back setting.

Staff T-Shirts ($3,000): Every staff member receives a free T-shirt
at the beginning of the year. We put a lot of thought into these
T-shirts, including asking staff to vote on their favorite design
and paying a couple extra dollars per shirt to get the ultra-soft
version (*BELLA+CANVAS*® brand is a district favorite!).

Flower Deliveries ($1,000): On the first day of school, we ask
our local florist to deliver plants to every new teacher/certified
employee. Each plant comes with a specially designed pot with
our school district logo. These gifts look great in classrooms and
help new staff feel special.

Special Delivery: These school-themed plants are a hit with teaching staff.

Popcorn Fridays ($1,000): We purchased a popcorn machine for each school so that staff could enjoy a salty snack each Friday morning. Not only does fresh popcorn smell amazing, we have found this simple gesture goes a long way toward making crazy Friday mornings more bearable.

Family Movies ($1,000): Staff are always looking for something to keep their kids entertained during summer and winter break. To help give our families something to do, we collaborate with our community theatre to host a free "staff-appreciation movie" for kids, grandkids, and spouses twice a year.

Yeti Mugs ($500): Our district emphasizes lifelong learning, so staff who earned a master's degree over the previous school year are given a special Yeti tumbler with our school logo engraved.

STC STAFF APPRECIATION CELEBRATION

Free Movie for all STC Staff
Dr. Seuss' "The Grinch"

Bring your kids, grandkids & spouses
Concessions will be available for a cost

Friday, December 28th at 10:00am
(During Winter Break)

The Wieting Theatre – S Church St, Toledo, IA

Pro Tip: Let staff vote on the movie and the date of the showing.

Finding a gift that everyone likes can be difficult . . . but we found these trendy mugs to be universal winners!

Baby Onesies ($300): We believe every employee (or employee's spouse) should be recognized for the birth of a baby. So, we order school-district themed "onesies" to give away during all-staff celebrations. Some staff have said they want a baby just for the onesie (they are joking . . . I think!)

School-themed onesies are super cheap and cherished by staff.

Keep in mind these ideas are shared from a district perspective. Building leaders can use a similar rule of thumb for their buildings: For every 100 students, invest $1,000 of your building budget into employee culture.

Work in a 500-student elementary school? Invest $5,000. Work in a 1,500-student high school? Invest $15,000. Of course, you could go much higher if you wanted, but these numbers reflect an investment that is a fraction of a percent compared to the overall building budget.

■ ■ ■

"How are you able to do those cool things for staff? I didn't think we could spend money on those items."

Let's address this question from two perspectives: district leadership and building leadership.

District Leaders: When I began my first year as a superintendent, I was told "staff-morale" purchases such as food, clothing, prizes, and other "swag" were not allowed. However, I also knew that other districts were making these purchases without issue.

As I researched this topic, a breakthrough occurred when I learned that auditors—the people who review and verify the accuracy of financial records—defer to *school board policy* when validating school purchases. Specifically, each district has an *"Expenditures for Public Purposes"* policy that governs allowable uses of school funds. Therefore, for our district to have flexibility on culture-building purchases, our public purpose policy needed modification.

Curious what my options were, I accessed sample board polices from the Iowa School Board Association (IASB) and the Iowa School Finance Information Services (ISFIS), searching for language that provided spending flexibility. I was happy to discover that these sample policies were far more flexible than our current policy.

One of the most helpful phrases came from ISFIS's sample policy and reads as follows: *"The Board of Directors authorizes the expenditures of Districts funds for . . . Motivational items for employees that align with the Board's mission and vision for teaching and learning and enhance the climate and culture of the district."*

Once drafted, the updated policy went to the school board for approval. Three key ideas were used as rationale during this discussion. First, I showed how the updated policy language came straight from state association guidance. Second, I shared research that spoke to the positive correlation between tokens of appreciation and employee retention.[3] Third, I explained that less than 1% of our general fund budget would be spent on these purchases.

After a short discussion, our board approved the new policy with a 5–0 vote.

Our full Expenditures for Public Purpose policy can be found on the South Tama County School District website. However, there are a few pieces of language I'd like to highlight:

> *The Board of Directors authorizes the expenditure of District funds . . . which aids in recruitment of personnel, promotes improvement of staff morale and cooperation, and assists in building a commitment to the District, thus assisting in creating a more productive learning environment.*

> *Staff appreciation meals (breakfast and/or lunch) to recognize employee contributions . . .*

> *Motivational items for employees that align with the Board's mission and vision for teaching and learning and enhance the climate and culture of the district, provided the items are of modest expense.*

District leaders should look at their current public purpose expenditures policy. If current language doesn't provide latitude, they should engage the school board in dialogue about modifying the language to allow for flexibility in spending.

■ ■ ■

Building Leaders: Similar to district leaders, building leaders should also investigate district policy. Far too often, building leaders don't take time to understand school board policy, and instead rely on district leaders to interpret procedural language. When administrators dig into policy, they often realize their supervisor is misinformed . . . whether it be about public purpose spending or other policy.

Another tip for school leaders is to compose a public purpose statement for staff purchases that may raise a red flag in your business office. Once the statement is written and printed, those documents should be paper-clipped to the receipt of the purchase in question.

Here is an example of a public purpose statement I've used in the past:

> *On Friday, August 23rd, the Tama Florist delivered an STC-themed pot and plant to all new certified STC employees. A total of 16 plants were delivered across all 4 buildings for a total cost of $770.40.*
>
> *I believe this purchase aligns with School Board Policy 804.07: Expenditures for Public Purpose. Specifically, I'd like to highlight the following statement: "Motivational items for employees that align with the Board's mission and vision for teaching and learning and enhance the climate and culture of the district, provided the items are of modest expense."*
>
> *My district credit card was used to make the purchase. Feel free to attach this email with the receipt in case the auditors have any questions.*

Here is another email I shared with our business office to justify purchasing T-shirts for employees:

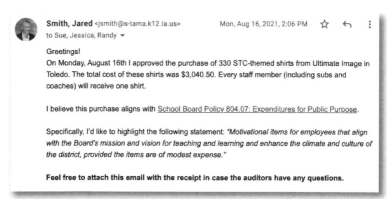

While not every purchase "gatekeeper" will be on board with your thinking, referring to school board policy and writing a public purpose statement helps build trust with the business department while reducing issues with auditors.

■ ■ ■

In a world where effective school personnel are hard to find, leaders must look for opportunities to show staff appreciation.

Whereas apathetic leaders shrug their shoulders and accept that it's "impossible" to use district funds for staff morale purchases, determined leaders push forward and insist that funds be used to invest in school culture.

GREAT LEADERS CREATE
MORE LEADERS

A couple of years ago I discovered that one of our administrators was being courted by a nearby district for an open position.

The neighboring district was three times our size, and the position would include increased responsibility and greater compensation. Despite being a promotion for the employee, my initial reaction was frustration.

"Those jerks!" I thought upon realizing a nearby district was recruiting one of our top employees. *"Who do they think they are?"*

My frustration also focused on our employee. *"What, are we not good enough for her?"* I complained. *"Besides, how are we going to find a suitable replacement in June?"*

However, I quickly realized that I was being selfish. Rather than focus on our organization, I was stressing over the actions of another school district. And rather than do what was best for our employee, I was worried about the additional work that would fall on my shoulders.

As leaders, it is our responsibility to help employees reach their full potential. Rather than feel threatened or betrayed when we discover they are ready to move on, our role is to help staff take their next professional step.

As leaders, our job is to create more leaders.

■ ■ ■

In *Multipliers*, Liz Wiseman says, *"The best leaders encourage people to grow and leave. And when people leave, they celebrate their departures and shout their success to everyone."*[4]

Consider your current school district:

Does your district encourage professional growth?
Or, does your district hinder leadership potential?

Unfortunately, many school leaders feel cheated when they realize an employee is leaving for another district. Rather than understand this is the next step in their professional career—or reflect on the steps they could have taken to make the individual feel more valued—these leaders immediately blame the employee: *"Well, they obviously weren't committed to our school,"* they tell others.

In the story I shared above, the employee would move from a director position into an assistant superintendent role. Accompanying the promotion would be a 40% salary increase. *Would you turn down a 40% salary increase?*

But say the employee makes a lateral move. Instead of moving up the leadership chain, what if the employee accepts a similar position in a new school district? These are situations when leaders must self-reflect. Rather than get mad at the person for leaving or blame another district, bosses should reflect on their treatment of the individual:

Have I offered support, or have I ignored requests for help?
Have I provided autonomy, or have I micromanaged their work?
Have I invested time, or have I been too busy for the employee?

Ironically, more employees leave jobs as a result of the relationship with their boss than they do their level of salary.[5]

> Leadership is about people.
>
> It's not about plans.
> It's not about programs.
> It's not about strategies.
>
> When you invest in people, the plans, programs, and strategies take care of themselves.
>
> #TurningPoints

Many district leaders threaten, *"You've signed a contract, you can't leave!"* when employees consider bolting for another job late in the hiring season. The truth is—at least here in Iowa—employees have until June 30th to get out of their contract without facing licensure repercussions.

This idea of districts intentionally sabotaging leadership growth does not always pertain to external movement. Sadly, many districts are guilty of stifling internal leadership potential.

One common example is when districts prevent their best assistant principals from moving into head principal roles. In many districts, up-and-coming assistant principals are serving under mediocre head principals. Rather than move the AP into a head principal role elsewhere in the district or—*heaven forbid*—remove the mediocre principal, district leaders keep gifted assistant principals in supporting roles for far too long.

Publicly, district leaders will say, *"Oh, they're just not ready for a head role,"* while privately they think, *"If we move them into a new position, their (current) school will fall apart!"* Rather than promote internal candidates, districts tell promising assistant principals, *"Your time will come"* while keeping them in the same role year after year.

While some gifted leaders will ignore the politics and patiently wait for their turn, others will grow tired of being underestimated and leave the district. Quite often, these individuals turn the disrespect into motivation and have highly successful careers.

■ ■ ■

What else should be considered with leadership development? Consider these five ideas:

Hire for Talent: Many leaders get scared about hiring highly talented individuals. Afraid the employee will leave after a couple years, they pass over the more-gifted candidate to select the safer fit. *This thinking is misguided.* Leaders should always hire the most qualified candidate and then offer opportunities for growth and autonomy. In many instances, school leaders simply want to work in a district where they feel trusted and valued.

They Might Take My Job: Egotistic leaders sometimes worry that understudies are so good in their roles they could eventually find themselves without a job. Rarely—if ever—does this scenario actually unfold in education. Not only are districts notorious for not moving underperforming leaders, if a go-getter lights a fire under a complacent leader . . . is this really a bad thing?

Next Man (or Woman) In: The fate of the district leader depends on the effectiveness of the school leaders they employ. Therefore, the best superintendents keep a shortlist of individuals—both internal and external—they can contact when leadership opportunities arise. Rather than sit back and wait for candidates to apply, cunning district leaders treat leadership openings like gold and aggressively recruit potential replacements.

Promote from Within: In *Good to Great*, Jim Collins reminds us, *"Visionary companies have shown, time and again, that they do not need to hire top management from the outside in order to get change and fresh ideas."*[6] How often have you seen school districts hire flashy outsiders . . . only to see those individuals leave in a few short years? Oftentimes, internal candidates possess limitless potential and simply need the right opportunity to shine.

Focus on Skills: Promoting an internal candidate can be a leap of faith. Oftentimes, colleagues struggle to imagine teachers in an administrative role. Rather than worry about "lack of experience," decision-makers should consider character traits. Does this person work hard and follow through on commitments?

Does this person have the respect of staff and build relationships with students? Quite often, the evidence is there. You just need to know where to look.

■ ■ ■

To no one's surprise, our administrator accepted the promotion in the nearby district.

Rather than get upset about the situation, I felt at peace knowing this individual was fulfilling her potential by having a greater impact in a larger district. Furthermore, I was confident that our district's reputation would allow us to recruit an effective leader to fill the position.

The Power of Rounding

I've had the opportunity to connect with several school leaders over the past few years.

During these conversations, my goal is to come away with at least one new idea that I can try in my own setting. To help meet this goal, I often ask the following: *"What is one professional practice that you would recommend to others?"*

This prompt has produced numerous great ideas that I now use, including sending birthday postcards to students, developing a communication protocol, encouraging "discipline on wheels," and journaling daily gratitudes.

However, one practice has produced the biggest return on investment: *Rounding Meetings.*

▪ ▪ ▪

In *The Effective Manager*, Mark Horstman proposes the following: *"The single most important (and efficient) thing you can do as a manager to improve your performance and increase retention is to spend time getting to know your direct reports."*[9]

Unfortunately, many school leaders do everything *but* spend time with their staff. Rather than connect with their people, school leaders send emails, supervise hallways, handle discipline, return phone calls, complete reports . . . and send more emails. To be clear, these are all important parts of school leadership. However, leaders cannot forget *the single most* important part of leadership: *employees.*

"This isn't my issue," you may be thinking. *"I talk to my people all the time."*

Yes, many school leaders are in constant communication with their direct reports through email, text, and face-to-face conversation. In fact, some school leaders "talk" to their employees so much that they hardly have time for their own work!

However, most school leaders have no idea how *one-sided* those conversations are. Walking up to an employee and saying, *"Hey, got a minute?"* does not count as "talking" with employees. Why? Because these conversations are driven by the leader's agenda.

"But I'm super friendly!" you may be thinking. *"I always ask how the wife and kids are doing are before asking my question!"*

Regardless of your small-talk skills, impromptu chats with staff do not build deep, meaningful relationships. Furthermore, spontaneous conversations rarely produce feedback from employees that push an organization forward.

Enter rounding meetings.

Rounding can be traced back to the health-care field. Rounding is when doctors "make the rounds" to see how patients are doing. These conversations are ideal for patients to discuss their recovery progress and to critique the medical care received. Although simple, physicians have found rounding to be especially helpful because conversations are focused on the *patient*.

The success of rounding in health care has led to extensive implementation in the business world. Rather than visit patients, CEOs, VPs, and managers check in on the status of their employees. During these discussions, supervisors ask how the employee is doing, what issues need to be addressed, and what supports the person needs to be successful. Most important, conversations are focused on the *employee*.

Unfortunately, rounding meetings have been slow to work their way into schools. Whereas many school leaders say, *"I check in with my staff all of the time,"* they fail to realize that—at their core—these conversations are dictated by the leader and rarely focus on improving the employee experience.

■ ■ ■

Curious to give rounding meetings a try in my setting, I committed to completing one 20-minute check-in conversation with every certified employee in our district. When I told my secretary, Jess, my plans, she looked at me a little funny: *"You want to set up meetings . . . with 130 employees?"*

Understand that my calendar is pretty scripted and full of routine meetings, including weekly 1:1 meetings that I complete with all ten of my direct reports. So, finding time to schedule so many conversations seemed aggressive.

"I know it sounds crazy, but we have the whole year," I assured her. *"Besides, I really want to hear what is going on in the trenches of*

our district. Do you think you can come up with a way to schedule these meetings? Pretty please?"

Jess playfully shook her head, wrote down a few notes, and assured me she would come up with something.

"I owe you big time!" I told her as she left my office.

Using *Calendly*, Jess gave staff access to my calendar and allowed them to pick a time that worked for their individual schedules, as well as a location for the meeting.

My next step was to create a set of questions to ask during each meeting. In speaking with others, I learned that *scripted questions*—as opposed to informal conversation—was a vital piece of the rounding process. Administrators only have a short amount of time with each employee, meaning that questions must be well-crafted to elicit productive conversation.

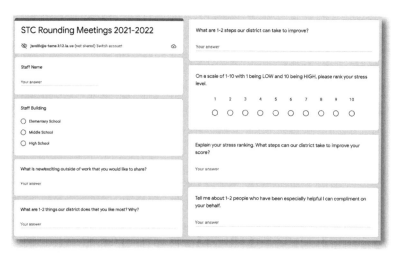

Once meetings were scheduled and questions were written, I was ready to begin. After only a few meetings, I began to realize the incredible impact of rounding meetings. Not only did I get to know each employee on a personal level, I also received great insight about the employee experience.

One of the biggest takeaways from my first 30 or so rounding conversations was the stress level of our teachers. Because these initial meetings occurred in September and October, I assumed staff would still be in the "honeymoon" period to start the year. So, I was shocked to discover how many employees were already reporting fatigue and burnout.

Armed with this surprising information, I went to our administrative team asking for solutions. Eventually, we approved a plan to add monthly two-hour early dismissals for teacher planning. When staff heard of these plans, they were ecstatic. Not only did they appreciate additional planning time, employees felt valued because school leadership responded to their feedback.

School Leaders:
Wise decisions don't happen by isolating yourself in an office.
Wise decisions happen by engaging with employees in the trenches.

#LearningCurve

Without rounding meetings, I would have lacked the insight to make this timely decision. Furthermore, the knowledge gained from rounding conversations gave me excellent perspective when discussing other topics with building leadership.

■ ■ ■

Thinking about trying rounding meetings in your setting? Here are seven ideas to consider:

No Pressure: Rounding meetings should start light, meaning bosses should encourage employees to share something new or exciting *outside* of work. While some staff may not say much, most employees will find *plenty* to talk about. These stories— whether they are about family, hobbies, or trips—are a great way to make the person feel comfortable and are valuable for future interactions.

Keep Notes: When employees are talking, I type notes directly into the Google Form. While some may worry this disrupts the intimacy of the conversation, I believe notes are essential because they allow me to revisit employee feedback at a later time. Furthermore, I share my notes with building administrators. This allows leaders to read positive feedback, as well as (appropriately) respond to any constructive criticisms.

Refine Questions: When I began, I asked the following: *"What do you like most about our district?"* Although this question was well-intentioned, I received answers such as *"I like the diversity"* and *"I like the size of the district."* While these were good answers, they did not speak to practices within our control. I found that *"What are 1–2 things our district does that you like the most?"* did a much better job of extrapolating meaningful and actionable feedback.

Build Trust: One of the most important parts of rounding meetings is asking staff to be honest about their workplace experience. In most cases, employees get nervous when sitting face to face with their boss. To put staff at ease, supervisors should use prompts such as: *"You can be honest—it won't hurt my feelings"* and *"The only way we get better is to know what is really going on"* to promote a safe environment and encourage employees to share their true feelings.

Dig Deeper: Once trust has been built, employees may voice frustrations with school leadership, coworkers, or the work environment. When they begin to share their grievances, many staff will pause to gauge their boss's reaction: *"Am I allowed to say this?"* they wonder. Administrators must notice this hesitation and encourage employees to keep sharing, as unearthing these insights constitutes the most valuable aspect of the rounding meeting.

Follow Through: As is the case with any meeting, conversation, or survey, bosses must be careful not to waste employees' time. If they don't feel like feedback is being used—*especially after sharing vulnerable feedback*—staff are less likely to trust administration in the future. Bosses must constantly search for opportunities to share how rounding feedback is being used. Team meetings, faculty meetings, and all-staff emails are perfect times for bosses to attribute building decisions to employee feedback.

Positive Feedback: The *"Tell me about 1–2 people who have been especially helpful I can compliment on your behalf"* question is my favorite part of the rounding process. After the meeting, I copy the positive feedback and paste it into an email template that is shared with both the person who was selected . . . as well as the person who gave the feedback. Quite often, I receive replies such as: *"this just made my day"* and *"you just made me tear up."* Talk about powerful!

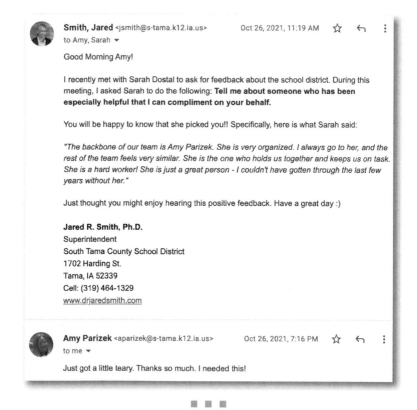

Smith, Jared <jsmith@s-tama.k12.ia.us>   Oct 26, 2021, 11:19 AM   ☆   ↩   ⋮
to Amy, Sarah ▾

Good Morning Amy!

I recently met with Sarah Dostal to ask for feedback about the school district. During this meeting, I asked Sarah to do the following: **Tell me about someone who has been especially helpful that I can compliment on your behalf.**

You will be happy to know that she picked you!! Specifically, here is what Sarah said:

"The backbone of our team is Amy Parizek. She is very organized. I always go to her, and the rest of the team feels very similar. She is the one who holds us together and keeps us on task. She is a hard worker! She is just a great person - I couldn't have gotten through the last few years without her."

Just thought you might enjoy hearing this positive feedback. Have a great day :)

Jared R. Smith, Ph.D.
Superintendent
South Tama County School District
1702 Harding St.
Tama, IA 52339
Cell: (319) 464-1329
www.drjaredsmith.com

Amy Parizek <aparizek@s-tama.k12.ia.us>   Oct 26, 2021, 7:16 PM   ☆   ↩   ⋮
to me ▾

Just got a little teary. Thanks so much. I needed this!

■ ■ ■

In a recent rounding meeting with a middle school teacher, I received the following feedback:

You have made it feel like you listen to all the teachers. You listen to what we say and you make the best judgment. You don't just sit in the office and make decisions. I've worked in four other districts and haven't seen this before. You actually listen and then make decisions—that's amazing.

Consider the decisions you make in your own setting.

Are you making arbitrary decisions from your office?
Or, are you making wise decisions based on staff feedback?

You're Not the Expert

On *The Group Project Podcast,* I interview school leaders from around the country. One of my favorite parts of the interview is asking guests to reflect on their biggest rookie mistakes.

Quite often I hear the same answer: *trying to be the expert at everything.*

On Episode #87 I interviewed Brent Barry, the Superintendent of the Phoenix-Talent School District in Oregon. In our interview, Barry reflected on his early struggles as a principal.

"My first year as an elementary principal, I felt like I had to be the expert at everything," said Barry, the Oregon Superintendent of the Year in 2022. *"I quickly learned I was wrong."*

"People were getting too dependent on me," Barry admitted. *"I couldn't possibly be the fixer of all problems. It was exhausting! After a while, I started thinking, 'Am I really the person who needs to solve that question? Or, do we have other people with more expertise who can solve that problem?'"*

"New leaders believe they have to be the go-to person for everything," Barry explained. *"That's just not possible. You can't possibly know everything about every subject area and every grade level."*

"Don't put the pressure on yourself to be the expert."

■ ■ ■

In 2016 I landed my "dream job." As the head principal of a building with 200 staff and 1,600 kids, I was asked to lead one of the largest high schools in Iowa.

At 34 years of age, I was the youngest-ever principal in this building. When I began, I heard words like *"I've been teaching longer than you've been alive"* and *"I'm old enough to be your mom"* from several employees.

Hearing this feedback made me feel good about my professional accomplishments. However, I also wanted to prove to staff that getting the job was no fluke. Although I was warned by mentors to *"take things slow"* . . . my ego begged me to show people *"what was up."*

So, I compromised: rather than make building-wide changes, why not focus on leadership-team changes? *"Certainly, our department chairs won't mind trying some new ideas,"* I figured.

Without asking for feedback or generating buy-in, I told our Building Leadership Team (BLT) we were changing many of our logistical processes: how often we met, when we met, the topics of conversation, and how we communicated.

"These changes will make us better," I explained. *"We did this in my previous school and it worked really well."*

While I didn't think these changes were a big deal, I quickly realized our leaders weren't ready. Almost immediately, I heard grumblings that BLT members were unhappy. When I asked my secretary what she thought the issue was, she provided some harsh feedback.

"They think you're moving too fast," she shared. *"They don't think you're listening to them."*

"Too fast? Not listening?" I rebutted. *"They are getting paid extra to be in these positions. Maybe they just need to suck it up!"*

"Hey, I'm just telling you what I'm hearing," she responded.

This standoff between myself and our BLT lasted months. Despite the fact that I was creating tension with key building leaders, my pride couldn't handle being wrong. *"If I change now, they won't respect me in the future,"* I worried.

While our team eventually adjusted to the changes, the damage was already done. I senselessly created adversarial relationships with several department chairs—relationships that took months to recover.

By stubbornly *telling* people what to do instead of *asking* people what to do, I was single-handedly sabotaging my leadership.

■ ■ ■

"The best leaders are great listeners," said James Kouzes and Barry Posner in *The Leadership Challenge*. *"They listen carefully to what other people have to say and how they feel. They ask good questions, are open to ideas other than their own, and even lose arguments in support of the common good."*[10]

Early in my career, I was told that leadership was about asking questions. At the time, that concept didn't make sense: *"How can I possibly lead if all I'm doing is asking questions?"*

It took ten-plus years in leadership to build the confidence and awareness to adopt a question-first mentality. But when I did, beautiful things started to happen.

First, I learned that asking questions empowered employees. When employees are asked to share their opinions on a topic, they feel valued and respected. And when employees are asked to give feedback on a decision, they are more likely to support the outcome.

Second, I learned that asking questions made my job easier. Early in my career, I believed it was my role to have all the answers—*to be the expert*—when employees approached me with concerns. However, I didn't realize I was inadvertently assuming the burden of the concern when I jumped in with answers as opposed to empowering employees to work through their issues.

"But shouldn't leaders assume responsibility?" you may be thinking. *"Isn't that 'servant' leadership?"*

Assuming they are not causing the issue (which is another topic all together), supervisors should help employees work through problems by asking questions as opposed to immediately providing answers.

Have you ever worked for an administrator who stubbornly demanded that all problems funnel through their office? While seemingly noble . . . in reality this approach creates a massive bottleneck in the organization where employees wait days (if not weeks) for issues to be solved.

In short, bosses don't have the bandwidth to shoulder responsibility for every decision within an organization. Rather than be the only source of answers, leaders must empower employees to make their own choices.

■ ■ ■

Research suggests that the best leaders spend 80% of the time listening and only 20% of the time talking.[11] Consider your conversations: How would you break down your time spent talking versus listening? Unfortunately, many school leaders struggle with this concept.

Several books provide ideas to improve listening through the use of effective questioning. One of the best is *The Coaching Habit* by Michael Bungay Stanier.[12] In his book, Bungay Stanier outlines several simple—yet effective—questions to guide employee conversations. Here are five of my favorites:

"What's On Your Mind?" This question is an easy way to begin any conversation with an employee. By asking this question (I also ask, *"What's going on in your world?"* and *"What's new with you?"*), leaders make it clear that the focus is on the *employee.* The open-endedness of this inquiry gives subordinates complete control over where the conversation goes next.

"And What Else?" Staff aren't used to being asked what is on their mind by the boss. Therefore, the likelihood that staff share what is *really* "on their mind" is slim. Leaders must encourage employees to share what is nagging at their conscience for the purpose of surfacing *real* issues—which are often thorny relationship issues and power struggles deep within the organization.

"What Do You Think is the Real Issue?" Employee conversations often jump from topic to topic. While this isn't a bad

thing (remember—you're *listening*—not telling), it's important for leaders to help guide employees to the root cause of their frustration. Rather than speaking in generalities, this question gives employees opportunities to share specific concerns.

"What Do You Want?" Given that they tend to focus on what others need, educators rarely come out and share what *they* need. Similarly, it is criminal how rarely supervisors genuinely ask employees what they need. Leaders who ask this question not only make employees feel valued, but also they build much stronger relationships with those individuals.

"How Can I Help?" This question encourages employees to make a clear request while preventing bosses from offering their own solutions. Oftentimes, leaders will hear employee complaints and immediately begin to address the issue. Unfortunately, this approach can backfire as most employees want to avoid drama with colleagues. Only after the employee has given their blessing should a boss address a problematic situation.

One last thought: These questions only work for leaders who have already established a culture of trust and vulnerability. Unless they work hard to rebuild their social capital, leaders who lack integrity will find it difficult to elicit honest feedback from employees.

■ ■ ■

Steve Jobs famously said, *"It doesn't make sense to hire smart people and tell them what to do; we hire smart people so they can tell us what to do."*

It took me far too long to realize leadership gets much easier when you quit trying to be the expert.

Don't make my same mistake.

Stop *telling* employees what to do.
Start *asking* employees what to do.

School Leaders:

Don't hire smart teachers and then tell them what to do.

Instead, hire smart teachers and ask them what to do.

#TurningPoints

You're Not Like Other Superintendents

"You're not like other superintendents."

Whereas you may have assumed this feedback was positive in nature, these words were actually the constructive criticisms I received a couple years ago from two employees.

During two separate conversations, I was questioned about work priorities. Rather than focus my time on "typical" superintendent tasks such as finances, facilities, and policy, these employees were curious as to why I delegated so much of this work to others.

"I just haven't worked with someone like you before," said one staff member, insinuating that I was neglecting these important tasks.

Like any critical feedback, I was upset for a couple days. *"Do they have any clue how far our district has come?"* I thought to myself. *"Fine . . . let's go back to the 'old' way of doing things!"*

However, I now realize it's unfair to blame them for having these opinions. Superintendents have long been viewed as the authority on finances, facilities, policy, and other managerial tasks. And while some leaders have successfully redefined those expectations . . . most superintendents are still viewed as the "face" of noninstructional departments.

■ ■ ■

"But if a superintendent doesn't focus on finances, facilities, and policy . . . then who will?"

Most school districts have individuals whose job is to oversee these branches of the district. Often referred to as "directors," these individuals manage departments such as food service, technology, custodial/maintenance, finance, and transportation. Similar to principals running a school building, directors are responsible for supervising staff, allocating resources, and managing their divisions in such a way that supports systemic operations.

However, conventional school leadership models have hindered the autonomy in these offices. Rather than empower directors to have ownership of their departments, many superintendents stubbornly insist on getting deep in the weeds of these auxiliary offices.

For example, say the director of food service wants to purchase new commercial mixers for each kitchen. Whereas common sense would say trust your director to understand her department needs, some superintendents recall the Black Friday deal they got on their KitchenAid and haggle over the purchases.

Or, say the director of transportation wants to purchase propane-powered school buses as opposed to diesel-powered school buses. While trusting superintendents have faith that their directors understand the newest trends in busing, skeptical superintendents think their *Car and Driver* subscription makes them well-equipped to debate the decision.

If you can't already tell, I'm baffled as to why district leaders waste time questioning their directors. These individuals were hired because they are experts in their field. *Let them do their job!* Besides, if directors can't be trusted to make basic decisions . . . then why are they still working in your organization?

Speaking of purchases, for years superintendents have been seen as the district finance authority. Even though schools have highly skilled business employees who are fully capable of being the "point people" for financial matters, traditional education practices suggest that the superintendent should be the finance gatekeeper.

While superintendents should certainly have a baseline knowledge of finances, is this where a school leader should be spending most of his or her time? Consider John Hattie's renowned *Effect Size Research*. On his list of 256 influences related to student achievement, Finances sits way down at 185—one spot below Visual/Audio-Visual Methods (184) and just a handful of spots above . . . Breastfeeding (227).[7]

Rather than spend time trying to understand every detail of school finance, shouldn't superintendents' time be spent on more impactful practices such as building teacher self-confidence (Hattie's number 1), monitoring the implementation of intervention programs (5), and addressing underperforming staff (12)?

▨ ▨ ▨

If district leaders wish to flip the script on their assigned duties, there are several steps they must take to ensure the transition goes smoothly. Here are five ideas to consider:

No Surprises: One of the most important things district leaders must do is share their leadership values and priorities with the school board *prior to accepting the job.* If a superintendent has a fondness for finance and facilities, great! But if not, they must be honest with the board during the interview process. While it can be tempting to tell the board what they want to hear, in the long run philosophical misalignment is a recipe for disaster.

Empower Staff: Noninstructional directors must be trusted to make their own decisions. Rather than be micromanaged by controlling supervisors, directors must be authorized to make wise decisions given their extensive knowledge and background. Furthermore, directors should be the *spokesperson* for their departments. As opposed to doing all of the talking, superintendents must empower directors to take on speaking and decision-making duties in meetings and other public forums.

Accountability: While most directors appreciate this "hands off" mentality, some directors will abuse this freedom. Bosses who notice recurring department issues—such as frequent complaints, high employee turnover, and lack of follow through—must hold leadership accountable. The best way to hold department leadership responsible is by scheduling weekly check-in meetings where updates are shared and commitments are made.

Define Roles: One of a leader's most important duties is to clarify the job responsibilities for the employees they supervise. Leaders who fail to perform this basic, yet important task create unnecessary confusion among employees which can lead to organizational dysfunction. Reflecting on the constructive feedback I received from our two employees, it was obvious that I had not spent enough time engaged in this process.

Systemic Communication: Once the director's job duties are defined, leaders must share this information with the entire organization. Transparent communication of roles establishes a clear chain of command while reducing harmful politics; few things damage a school more than power struggles over job responsibilities.

One of a leader's most important duties is to clarify the job responsibilities for the employees they supervise.

Leaders who fail to perform this basic, yet important task create unnecessary confusion among employees which can lead to organizational dysfunction.

#TurningPoints

■ ■ ■

In *The 8th Habit,* Stephen Covey shares:

> *If you study the underlying roots of almost all communication breakdowns or broken cultures, you'll find they come from either ambiguous or broken expectations around roles and goals; in other words, who is to do what role and what are the high priority goals of those roles.*"[8]

For decades, superintendents have been viewed as experts on finance, facilities, and policy. However, as more instructionally minded leaders enter the profession, the superintendent's role is likely to experience momentous change in the coming years.

Progressive superintendents cannot underestimate how these adjustments will impact stakeholders who are used to traditional methods of district leadership. Rather than assume employees will automatically understand their leadership priorities, superintendents must commit time to discuss, define, and communicate these changes.

Too Many Cooks in the Kitchen?

"You don't want too many cooks in the kitchen!"

This phrase is used to suggest when too many people work on the same project, the quality of the final product suffers as a result.

As I moved up the leadership chain, other leaders used this phrase to justify why they made decisions in isolation or with a small inner circle. Assuming other leaders knew what they were talking about, I adopted this mental model.

The following are times I believed *less was more* when it came to staff input:

Grading Policies: *"People get so heated! Let's use a small group."*
Student Handbook: *"We can figure it out as an admin team."*
MTSS/RTI: *"The less people involved in planning . . . the better!"*
Interviews: *"Having a big committee will only complicate things."*
Scheduling (Block vs. Periods): *"Let's just ask department chairs."*

In each instance, I believed having a select group of individuals at the table would allow us to make the best decision in the shortest amount of time. Furthermore, by shutting out the voices of other staff—some of whom would bring conflicting opinions—I figured we would avoid unnecessary decision-making drama.

I now realize this approach was ill-advised.

Because they were not involved in the process, staff felt little commitment to decisions that were made. And when marching orders hit snags in the road—as all five examples did—frontline employees were not motivated to actively search for solutions.

"No one asked me," staff would explain. *"I could have told you that wouldn't work."*

■ ■ ■

Revisiting *Multipliers* (see page 14), Liz Wiseman shares the following:

> *When leaders play the role of decision maker, they carry the burden of making the right decision and carrying it through to completion. This can be a heavy burden. But when the leader engages a team in making a decision, they distribute this load to the team. Having worked through the issues, the team will put their full weight behind the decision.*

When you make decisions, where does the burden fall?

Bosses who make decisions alone or with a small inner circle play a risky game. Of course, when decisions are correct leaders come out looking pretty smart. However, when decisions are wrong, leaders who have not generated buy-in with staff immediately assume burden of the decision. Not only do people question the decision, employees also lose trust in the leader's ability to make wise decisions moving forward.

Rather than make decisions in isolation, leaders must include others in the process. Research shows that diversity of opinions leads to better decision-making.[13] Administrators who actively engage faculty with diverse perspectives generate a comprehensive perspective on the problem. Furthermore, when staff are asked for input, they are far more likely to support the plan when things get difficult.

"I don't need to worry about this," some readers may be thinking. *"I always include others in decisions."*

While many bosses believe they promote a culture of collaborative decision-making, research proves otherwise. One recent study indicates that 80% of leaders believe they actively seek employee input on decisions, whereas only 10% of employees believe they are "fully empowered" to help make critical decisions.[14]

If your school or district were surveyed, would this same disconnect occur?

Another important thing to understand is that today's employees want to be a part of the decision-making process. According to *Forbes* Magazine, younger workers *"expect their views to be noticed and acted upon"* at work.[15] And rather than blindly follow directives—as was the case in previous generations—modern employees want to understand why decisions are made.

"I'm sick of younger employees being 'unhappy' at work," some leaders complain. *"They need to stop whining and understand that life doesn't always revolve around them."*

While this sounds reasonable, school leaders must realize that the balance of workplace power has shifted. Thanks to a historic imbalance of supply and demand, employees now hold unprecedented leverage on employers and will bolt when they don't believe their voice is being heard.

■ ■ ■

Looking to improve collaborative decision-making but not sure where to start? Consider these seven ideas:

Explain the Process: When making a complex decision, leaders must tell staff how the decision will be made *before* the process begins. Who will be involved? How is feedback gathered? How long will the decision take? Bosses who invest time to explain the process encounter far fewer issues when a decision is made.

Ask For Feedback: For each decision, leaders must determine *"Who will be impacted by this decision?"* While not every staff member will be able to weigh-in on decisions, leaders must consult with those who are closest to the issue. Don't have the time to meet with several individuals? Online surveys, collaborative documents (e.g., Google Docs), and email help with efficiency.

Leverage Feedback: Have you ever worked for a leader who asked for feedback . . . but then never explained how the feedback was used? Bosses must get in the habit of reporting how employee feedback drives decisions. This practice is especially powerful when feedback aligns with the decision being made.

All Means All: When decisions are made in a group setting, it is important that *all* voices are heard. Too often, teams will look at the person in the room with the most influence (or the loudest voice) and follow his or her lead. Leaders must create an environment where all staff are encouraged to voice their honest opinions, even if those opinions differ from the group.

Breaking Ties: When feedback reveals a clear winner, leaders would be wise to make the decision that mirrors the feedback. But what happens when there is no clear solution? This is when leaders must fulfill one of their most important responsibilities: *breaking ties.* Again, leaders who explain this process ahead of time eliminate unnecessary split-decision drama.

Divergent Opinions: What if the group shares a collective opinion that differs from the leader? In most cases, leaders would be wise to yield to the group. While there will be moments when leaders must go against the grain . . . these instances should be rare. Leaders who adopt a "disagree and commit" mindset (discussed at length in *Learning Curve*) build trust and earn the respect of colleagues.

Communicate the Decision: Once a decision is made, leaders must articulate the decision to the broader audience. If the decision was complex or heated, leaders are advised to explain how the decision was made. In terms of communicating the decision, face-to-face (opportunities for employee questions) and email (clear documentation of the decision) both offer advantages. In a perfect world, leaders explain the decision in person and then follow up with a detailed email.

■ ■ ■

I'll admit: I used to *hate* inviting cooks into the kitchen. Not only does asking others for feedback make the decision-making process longer, it increases the likelihood that my idea won't be selected.

However, I now realize those drawbacks are nothing compared to dealing with the aftermath of a bad decision.

School leaders must eliminate *"You don't want too many cooks in the kitchen"* from their vocabulary. Instead, we must actively seek input from those who are impacted by a decision to ensure their opinions are being heard.

EVERY DAY IS BOSS'S DAY

Regardless of your position in a school district, you will always report to someone:

Teachers report to an administrator.
Administrators report to a superintendent.
Superintendents report to a school board.

And regardless of supervisor, there are always tasks to complete. Whether it's completing paperwork, collecting information, or creating presentations, meeting a boss's expectations is a way of life.

When a supervisor asks you to complete a task, how do you respond?

Does the request become a top priority?
Or, does the request fall through the cracks?

While addressing the needs of peers and direct reports is important, few things matter more than how you respond to the demands of a direct supervisor.

■ ■ ■

47

In *The Principal: Surviving and Thriving*, Andrew Marotta discusses the importance of meeting a supervisor's expectations. Consider the following:

> *Take care of items and issues for your bosses right away. You cannot miss your boss's stuff. Replying to emails, attending meetings, dealing with things. In spite of whatever is flying at you, make sure you see and tend to your boss's stuff. If you miss a couple times, they will start to doubt you and lose trust in you.*[16]

While meeting a supervisor's expectations seems like a no-brainer, many school leaders struggle with this concept. Whether it's a missed deadline, incomplete paperwork, or an unanswered email, some school leaders have a habit of making life difficult for their boss.

"What difference does it make it if comes from a boss, a peer, or a direct report?" you may be thinking. *"Isn't everyone important?"*

While responding to requests from peers and direct reports is important, replying to a supervisor's request is more important. Why? *Because your boss determines your professional fate.* While others' opinions play a role in your success, your supervisor is the only person responsible for measuring your job performance.

"Yeah, but what if your boss is unreasonable?" you may wonder. *"My boss sucks."*

Working for an unreasonable boss is a whole different issue and deserves its own chapter. While the rest of this section assumes you work for a halfway competent boss, understand there is a silver lining for anyone who is stuck with a horrible supervisor: you learn what *not* to do. Great leaders often use these personal adversities as a source of motivation . . . vowing never to put others in similar circumstances.

Finally, take comfort in knowing that your time will come. Given the mass exodus of people leaving educational leadership, those who commit to professional development and lifelong learning will have their pick of jobs in the coming years.

> Given the mass exodus from the field, educational leaders who commit to professional development and lifelong learning will have their pick of jobs in the coming years.
>
> #TurningPoints

Assuming your boss is halfway competent, let's continue.

As a general rule, approximately 90% of employees regularly meet their boss's requests. Assuming bosses have reasonable expectations, most employees meet those demands without issue. However, what about the other 10% of employees? What about staff who struggle to meet supervisor expectations?

Consider your school for a moment. Are there teachers who can't be trusted to update grades, turn in paperwork, or call back parents? Whether they lack organizational skills—or think a boss's orders are unimportant—these individuals cannot be trusted to complete even the simplest of tasks.

Beyond teachers, many school leaders also struggle meeting supervisor demands. Although we assume administrators are inherently dependable, some administrators struggle more than teachers. Whether they fail to upload a report, document a conversation, or respond to an email, each district has leaders who cannot be trusted.

I once supervised a leader who constantly missed deadlines and failed to follow through on commitments. Regardless of task, I always knew I needed to watch this employee to ensure duties were completed.

As a leader who preaches, *"Assume the positive!"* and encourages workplace autonomy, having a weak link on our team was maddening. Whereas I could trust other team members to complete tasks without worry, I spent considerable time and energy asking for missing work and reinforcing expectations with this individual.

After a few years of working with this employee, I realized our partnership could not last. I was spending far too much time managing this (highly-paid) employee as opposed to doing my own work.

Eventually—using the steps outlined on page 139—this leader was removed. While dismissing an employee is hard work, replacing subpar leaders with strong performers is vitally important. Making leadership "upgrades" not only allows you to get your work done, it eliminates the stress felt by managing a poor employee.

Consider the leaders you supervise:

Is there someone who struggles taking direction?
Is there someone who creates more harm than good?
Is there someone you can't trust to get the job done?

Few things limit a school's potential more than inept leadership.

■ ■ ■

Let's face it: moving up the school leadership ladder is a bit of a game. As much as we wish promotion was straightforward and merit-based, politics and posturing will always play a role.

One of the quickest ways to master the game is by ensuring your boss's work is done at a high level. Here are five key ideas to consider:

Capture: Employees must have a reliable system to track commitments. Whereas some leaders stubbornly rely on memory to recall responsibilities, efficient leaders develop a system for keeping track of duties. Notecards, Post-it notes, and electronic documents are all great places to start. I prefer using a 5" x 8.25" Moleskine Notebook to track my to-do list (see page 206).

Communicate: One surefire way to lose your boss's trust is poor communication. High-functioning bosses demand effective communication from direct reports. Whether it be email, text, or phone call, employees must respond to their supervisor in a timely manner . . . or quickly find themselves in hot water.

Clarify: School leaders are very busy, meaning sometimes they don't define what they need from direct reports. As discussed in *Learning Curve*, highly effective employees seek clarity by asking "dumb questions." Rather than guess what the boss is wanting, ask questions to ensure tasks are done correctly.

Control: School leaders must learn how to effectively manage the day-to-day responsibilities of their position. From a superintendent's perspective, few things are better than principals who "keep their house in order" by limiting the major issues that leak from their building. Looking for a fast way to promotion? Learn how to put out fires before they reach your supervisor's desk.

Check-In: Direct reports who want to ensure they are meeting their boss's demands may want to request a recurring 1:1 meeting with their supervisor. Employees who initiate these alignment conversations not only build relationships, they also hold their boss accountable for clarifying job duties and expectations.

■ ■ ■

National Boss's Day is celebrated annually on October 16th.

On this day, employees give bosses cards, flowers, and presents.

While all are nice gestures, most bosses would gladly trade employee gifts for employee dependability.

Rather than celebrate Boss's Day once a year, start treating *every day* like Boss's Day.

No Surprises

When I accepted my first job as school superintendent, I wasn't sure what to expect. To prepare for the role, I reached out to several current and former superintendents asking for advice.

While arranging these conversations took work, the advice gleaned during these discussions was absolute *gold*. We covered many topics including administrator evaluation, program assessment, instructional leadership, and public relations.

However, one particular conversation will always stand out. During a phone call with a retired superintendent, I asked him to share his best school leadership "rule of thumb." When I asked him the question, he paused for a moment, and then said the following:

"No surprises."

After another pause, he continued:

When facing a major issue, you must keep the board and your administrators in the loop. You must guarantee they are never caught off guard, and you must avoid making decisions that leave them scratching their heads. In turn, they should limit their surprises as well. It all comes down to no surprises . . . you must create a culture of no surprises.

In theory, the concept of "no surprises" sounds simple.
In practice, creating a culture of "no surprises" is far from easy.

■ ■ ■

Surprises come in all shapes and sizes and originate at all levels
of school leadership. Surprises typically start with a leader saying
"By the way . . ." and end with an unexpected request or demand.
Examples include:

". . . you have an IEP meeting today after school."
". . . you will teach a new course second semester."
". . . you have a student teacher starting next week."
". . . you need to sell tickets at the game tonight."
". . . you have a new student starting today."
". . . you are moving buildings next year."

To administrators, these may not seem like big deals. *"Teachers
will just have to adjust"* principals declare prior to changing
teacher lunch schedules or implementing a new classroom
walkthrough template. While some staff go with the flow and
make adjustments, most employees do not appreciate surprises.

Consider the science behind surprises. According to *Surprise:
Embrace the Unpredictable and Engineer the Unexpected* by Tania
Luna and LeAnn Renninger, surprises magnify emotions by
as much as 400%.[17] When surprises are positive, the resulting
happiness feels four times stronger compared to the same event
without the surprise. Alternately, when surprises are negative,
the resulting unhappiness feels four times as intense.

This is where school leaders must be very careful. Whereas many
bosses believe their surprises will benefit staff, in reality they have

the opposite effect. *"Why wouldn't employees want to be recognized in front of the faculty?"* and *"Why wouldn't our at-risk team want another counselor?"* were two surprise decisions I made as a high school principal that didn't work so well.

As a high school assistant principal, I will never forget when we decided to hold a last-minute pep rally for our football team. Our team was in the middle of the 2012 state playoffs—and while we already held a pep rally for the first-round game—there was mounting student pressure to hold a pep rally for the second-round game.

Always a sucker for school spirit, I convinced our administrative team to cut 8th period by 20 minutes so we could gather in the gym to give our football team a fitting farewell. *"Why wouldn't teachers want to end class 20 minutes early?"* I assured the other administrators.

So as the last lunch shift wrapped up, I got on the loudspeaker and announced, *"By the way . . . we will have another pep assembly for our football team. Please bring your class to the gym at 2:40pm. Go Trojans!"*

Assuming I had made their day easier, I visited several classrooms shortly after the announcement. But instead of excitement, I noticed frustration on teachers' faces. *"I'm giving my 8th period a test. What am I supposed to do?"* asked one teacher. *"This is the third time you've shortened 8th period in the last two weeks,"* said another. *"You've had two pep assemblies for the football team, but nothing for our music programs,"* said a third.

The more classrooms I visited, the more I realized my "surprise" had backfired. What should have been a cool moment for our students was diminished because of added stress given to our teachers.

Front: Former NFL player JJ Moses hyping up the crowd.
Back: Me trying to get in the pep assembly "zone."

What steps can leaders take to limit surprises? Consider these five ideas:

Brainstorm: When decisions are imminent, cycle through every individual who could potentially be impacted by the news. Even seemingly small decisions—such as when meetings are scheduled or how to order classroom supplies—could create issues if leaders do not look at each decision through a *"who-could-be-surprised-by-this-news"* lens.

It Goes Both Ways: When limiting surprises, the natural tendency is to consider employees we supervise. However, school leaders must also consider their supervisors. As discussed in the previous chapter, whether you report to a principal, superintendent, or the school board . . . understand that *your boss determines your professional fate.*

Ask for Feedback: One simple step to avoid surprises is asking questions. *"What do you think about this idea?"* is a powerful question. Bosses who constantly ask employees for feedback on ideas eliminate the surprised feeling when decisions are made. Furthermore, leaders who actively pose questions and seek input find that staff are more supportive of decisions.

Don't Wait: Reduction in force. Plan of assistance. Realignment of duties. Administrators are responsible for having difficult conversations with employees. Fearful of upsetting their staff, many bosses wait until the last minute to share bad news. While some information must remain confidential, the general rule of thumb is the earlier you communicate and the more informed your people are, the better they'll be able to deal with discomfort.

Explain Tough Decisions: School leaders are notoriously bad when it comes to explaining tough decisions . . . especially personnel decisions. Rather than tell subpar employees why they are being moved to a different position or tell aspiring leaders why they didn't get a promotion, many bosses avoid these conversations all together. Not only is this approach unfair to the employee, this creates a culture of mistrust and uncertainty within the organization.

Apologize: Did you make a decision that took staff off guard? When this happens, one of the best things you can do is take ownership of the mistake. Apologizing is one of the most powerful gestures in the human arsenal. Leaders who have the courage to say, *"I'm sorry . . . I screwed up . . . I won't make the same mistake again,"* build trust with employees and can win over even the harshest of critics.

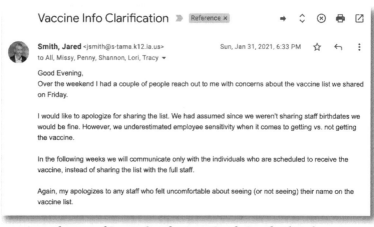

An apology email I sent after sharing a Google Doc that listed names of employees who planned to get the COVID vaccine. Whoops!

Having spent several years thinking about surprises, I've developed the following theory:

"People only get upset when they are surprised."

Think about this phrase for a moment. When you feel most upset, what are the root causes?

My son took the car without asking.
My daughter is failing a class.
My boyfriend cheated on me.
My girlfriend made plans during the game.
My husband forgot our anniversary.
My wife maxed out our credit card.
My friend isn't coming to my wedding.
My colleague didn't show up to work.
My boss is making me work this weekend.

In every case, what is the root cause of unhappiness? *Being surprised.*

Bosses who establish a culture of "no surprises" bring stability to a profession full of uncertainty.

WHAT HAVE YOU DONE
FOR ME LATELY?

Leaders across all professions now live in a world where they are judged with a *"what-have-you-done-for-me-lately"* mentality.

Rather than consider what they have done over the long term, bosses are now being judged on their most recent actions. Whereas these individuals may have a stellar professional track record, today's instant gratification culture shows them no mercy.

One prime example is college athletics. In the high-stakes world of college football, coaches can reach legendary status one year . . . and be fired the next.

Take, for instance, former Auburn Football Head Coach Gene Chizik. In just his second season at the helm, Chizik led his team to a 14–0 record and the 2010 National Championship. This was the first national title in *fifty-three years* for a football-crazed university. For many Tiger fans, Chizik was hailed as the Second Coming.

However, the next two seasons were not nearly as successful. In 2011, Chizik's Auburn team went 8–5. And in 2012, they went 3–9. As the end of the season neared, Auburn alumni grew restless. Fans who were once Chizik's most loyal supporters called for his firing.

Sure enough, *less than 24 hours* after the season ended, Chizik was terminated. Just two years removed from being named National Coach of the Year, Chizik was without a job.

Although their jobs may not be as high profile as college football coaches, many school leaders also fall victim to recency bias. School leaders can make incredible progress for years—but over time—stakeholders forget how far they've come and instead focus only on recent events.

Rather than feel bad for themselves or question their professional abilities, leaders must understand that today's society operates with a short-term memory.

■ ■ ■

For a moment, imagine a low-performing school with a history of underperformance. The school has gone through a number of principals due to poor hiring and a toxic environment. However, this time the school hires a dynamic principal. In just one short year, the principal brings new life to the building.

Employees say, *"We love working for our new boss!"*
Parents say, *"The new principal is awesome!"*
Board members say, *"We are happy to have them here!"*

Fast-forward to a few years later. The new leader "shine" has faded as people adjust to the new normal. Even though the principal has brought numerous positive changes . . . stakeholders begin to nitpick and question their effectiveness:

Staff say, *"School leadership doesn't listen to staff."*
Parents say, *"The principal should be doing more."*
Board members say, *"I'm not sure they fit our community."*

It's as if the dysfunction prior to the leader's arrival is completely forgotten.

While this narrative doesn't seem fair to the leader, this rapid decline in public opinion highlights a principle of human psychology called a*daptation.*

In *The Paradox of Choice*, Barry Schwartz explains, *"Adaptation means that as we get used to things, we start to take them for granted. Because of adaptation, enthusiasm about positive experiences doesn't sustain itself."*[18]

Adaptation is found in all aspects of life. For example, at some point you likely bought a new car. You loved everything about your new vehicle: the look, the smell, the features. Every time you thought about your car, you got excited.

However, over time the excitement wore off. As your car needed repairs and new cars hit the market, you began to take your vehicle for granted. A few short years later—if not sooner—you started to wonder if it's time to trade in your "old" car for something new.

Me in 2021: "I LOVE my new Jeep!!"
Me in 2022: "Meh . . . gets me from point A to point B."

Similar to how you treated your car over time, school districts treat their leaders the same way. Whereas the individual may be one of the best principals a building has ever had, over time staff and parents assume things would be better with someone else in charge.

■ ■ ■

One personal example occurred during winter a couple years ago.

When I took over the role of superintendent, I was told we needed to shore up communication around weather-related cancellations. Apparently, stakeholders were frustrated with the timeliness and transparency of previous decisions.

Immediately, I committed to improving these aspects of our winter-weather communication. Parents appreciated the early announcements so they could adjust their schedules, and staff valued the transparency in how we made decisions. For several years, we were applauded for these improvements.

However, on March 15th, 2021, we got caught in some untimely bad weather. As of 5:00am, roads were manageable and the forecast looked clear. After some discussion, we decided to bring kids into school. However—as kids were being dropped off—the weather quickly turned for the worst. And after checking with our district leadership team, we chose to cancel school for the day.

You would have thought the world was ending. Immediately, parents flooded the district with their displeasure on how the situation was handled.

They let their opinions be known through phone calls, emails, and—of course—social media.

Here is some of the "constructive feedback" we received on our Facebook page:

"Someone needs to pay attention . . ."
"This one is on you, STC administration!"
"Superintendent must have forgot to set his alarm."
"Your policies need to be ripped up."
"Roads were crap at 5:30!"
"Ridiculous!"

To make matters worse, I received word that several employees were upset with the decision.

"Staff are upset about this morning's communication," was one message I received.

"Did you think about your staff when you made your decision?" was another.

"We need to seriously consider changing our weather policies," was a third.

Some employees insisted that a complete overhaul of our communication processes—processes that were the envy of other communities—were needed.

While this is just one example, the truth is many stakeholders operate with recency bias. Whether the situation involves the handling of a thorny student issue—or the dismissal of a popular staff member—leaders who do great things *for years* can quickly find themselves in the doghouse.

■ ■ ■

What can leaders do to combat the *"what-have-you-done-for-me-lately"* mentality? Consider the following:

You Are Not Alone: Awareness of how humans behave is one of the best ways to cope with challenging situations. Understanding the concept of adaptation and realizing that humans have a tendency to lose enthusiasm about initially positive experiences can help school leaders not take things so personally.

Revisit the Good Times: Leaders are advised to remind others how far the school has come under their leadership. One of the best ways to accomplish this is by routinely sharing multiyear data trends with staff and the community. While presenting performance "evidence" may feel self-serving, these reminders prevent stakeholders from focusing solely on recent events.

STC Open Enrollment Trend

	2017-2018	2018-2019	2019-2020	2020-2021	2021-2022
Open Enrollment OUT	125	114	99	97	97
Open Enrollment IN	20	33	27	45	51
Open Enrollment NET	(-105)	(-81)	(-72)	(-52)	(-46)
Open Enrollment GAIN since 2017-2018		+24	+33	+53	+59

One example we use to remind our community of the progress we have made.

Turn the Tables: The good thing about recency bias is that it works both ways. Say a leader is criticized for being unapproachable. Rather than ignore the feedback and allege, *"They don't know what they're talking about,"* this leader should use recency bias to their *advantage* and take steps to being more accessible. Leaders who have the humility to admit their faults and work on their shortcomings can alter public perceptions in short periods of time.

Fresh Start: Few people want to show up to a job when their efforts go unrecognized. There are many reasons why principals average only four years in a position,[19] and feeling underappreciated is one of them. Many leaders indicate that moving to a new job where they feel valued can be a breath of fresh air and rejuvenate a career.

Buyer's Remorse: Assuming you treat your people with respect and perform your job to the best of your abilities, people who are critical of your work will eventually realize *"we didn't have it so bad"* when you are gone. Too many times, employees wish for another boss only to realize they made a huge mistake when the new leader is a dud. People who stay positive and lead with integrity leave lasting legacies in schools.

■ ■ ■

School leaders must understand that humans have short memories. In a fast-paced world where the only constant is change, people are wired to always be on the lookout for better options.

When employees complain about your leadership after years of effectiveness, don't beat yourself up. Instead, understand that even the greatest of leaders go through similar experiences.

Eventually, staff will realize they didn't have it so bad after all . . .

THE FACEBOOK FRIEND MYTH

For the longest time, school leaders have been advised to avoid being Facebook friends with employees.

"You don't want to get too close to your staff," veteran leaders warned.

For most of my professional life, I followed this advice. When employees sent friend requests, I ignored their advances. Careful not to hurt feelings, I never deleted requests . . . I simply let them sit idle until I left the district. Only after leaving would I accept the dozens of pending friend requests sitting in my inbox.

But when I became a superintendent, I used a different strategy. Rather than disregard the invitations, I began accepting friend requests from employees. *"Let's see how this goes . . ."* I thought upon accepting my first request from a current employee.

At first, only a few staff members reached out. But when others noticed I was accepting friend requests, the floodgates opened. Several years later, and I was Facebook friends with hundreds of current staff.

Whereas I was initially hesitant to change my philosophy, I now believe accepting employee friend requests—and engaging with those individuals online—is my best "secret weapon" for building workplace relationships.

■ ■ ■

Belgian psychotherapist Esther Perel said, *"Always take the time to acknowledge people. If you show interest in them, they will be interested in you."* [20]

For bosses who are looking to acknowledge and show interest in employees, few places are more efficient than social media. While in-person conversations still rule for building meaningful relationships, leaders cannot underestimate the power of social networking.

Social media—Facebook in particular—is where staff share what is most important in their lives. Whether they post pictures of a new grandchild, a wedding engagement, or a family vacation, when something important happens in their lives, staff spread the news on social media.

When you have hundreds of employees—like many school leaders do—it can be hard to keep tabs on the latest news. And while leaders don't need to know *everything* that goes on, Facebook provides quick snapshots of employee milestone moments.

What is particularly advantageous about Facebook friendships is that leaders have two distinct opportunities to make employees feel special. The first opportunity is when the leader initially scrolls through their feed and notices an employee post. When a leader "likes" the post and leaves a positive comment, this reinforces a people-first leadership approach.

"Wow, my boss commented on my post," employees think upon receiving notification. *"That really means a lot!"*

The second opportunity to make the employee feel special happens later when the leader crosses paths with the individual at work. Rather than engage in classic *"Good morning!"* or *"How are you?"* small talk, the boss can focus attention on the employee by saying, *"Your new puppy is so cute!"* or *"How did your 5K race go?"*

Another powerful aspect of Facebook friendships is that they help to eliminate traditional school "hierarchies." In many school settings, support staff feel overlooked and underappreciated. Some school leaders don't even know the names of these employees!

School leaders who engage with support staff on social media do wonders to build relationships with these individuals. In a time when quality paraeducators, custodians, bus drivers, secretaries, and food service personnel are hard to find, leaders should view Facebook as an opportunity to show interest in those employees while simultaneously increasing the likelihood that they stick around.

"Bosses shouldn't be Facebook friends with employees."

Baloney.

Leaders who prioritize relationships understand Facebook is a gold mine for discovering what is most important in the lives of employees.

#TurningPoints

"But I don't do social media," some readers may be thinking. *"It's a waste of time."*

I totally get it. Studies have found a strong link between heavy social media use and mental health issues such as anxiety and depression. Furthermore, the addictive nature of social media drains precious brainpower and robs us of time that could be spent on productive activities.

However, school leaders must understand current reality. Not only do 81% of American adults have Facebook accounts, 97% of college graduates use social media.[21] And while platforms change with time, social media shows no signs of slowing down.

The point is, Facebook is where employees congregate. While not all school leaders are fans of social media, most school employees *are*. And when school leaders say they *"don't do Facebook,"* they willingly forego valuable opportunities to positively engage with staff.

On the other hand, leaders who are open to social media realize that online friendships aren't all that complicated. When they carefully navigate potential social media landmines, leaders discover that Facebook provides untapped leverage for building relationships and enhancing workplace culture.

■ ■ ■

Thinking about taking this advice and accepting employee friend requests? Here are seven tips to remember:

Be Careful: It goes without saying that school leaders must be cautious about what they post. Social media blunders are one of the quickest ways for school leaders to get into trouble. In today's society, far more leaders are fired as a result of careless social media posts than they are low test scores.

Don't Play Favorites: Leaders must remember that some employees will attempt to read between the lines and dissect certain communications. Therefore, school leaders must remain relatively consistent in how they interact with employees. You certainly don't want to give off the impression that you favor certain staff.

One Way Street: While some may disagree, I am not a huge fan of bosses initiating friend requests. Not every employee wants to be chummy with their boss, and that is perfectly fine. Rather than put employees in an awkward situation, bosses should sit back and let staff members initiate friend requests.

Time Commitment: Adopting this professional practice shouldn't take much time. Most school leaders are already on Facebook, and dropping a like or leaving a comment on an employee's page takes only a few seconds. Five to ten minutes every couple of days is all that is needed for this practice to be impactful.

Return the Favor: School leaders who engage with employees on social media often notice that those individuals will reciprocate the support. Not only does it feel good when staff like your personal posts, school leaders typically find that employees with whom they have strong online relationships come to their defense when community members question school-related decisions.

Public Culture: Given that Facebook comments are visible to the public, leaders should treat each post as an opportunity to positively impact the broader school community. Leaders who are genuinely thoughtful, enthusiastic, and caring create an online presence that is infectious to others.

■ ■ ■

Managerial myth says that school leaders shouldn't become Facebook friends with employees.

Assuming you are professional on social media and are willing to invite others into your "personal" online space, it's time to set this myth aside.

School leaders who go from blocking invites to accepting requests can take relationship building to a whole new level.

It's Complicated

My first day as an assistant principal was a whirlwind.

The day began at the district office where I completed paperwork and met district-level personnel. Next, I drove to my building where I was met by the head principal. After briefly chatting, we walked into the main office where I was introduced to several employees, including the nurse, counselors, custodians, and secretaries.

After exchanging pleasantries and chatting for a few moments, I was escorted to my office. When I opened the door, I looked around in awe: *"Wow, I have my own office!"* I thought to myself. *"I've made it to the big time!"*

After looking around and taking in my surroundings, I plopped down in my fancy office chair and took a few deep breaths. *"What do I do next?"* I wondered.

It was during this time when I began thinking about my secretary. My first thoughts were, *"I can't believe I have my own secretary!"* At 26-years old, it was a surreal feeling knowing an employee's main role was to provide *me* with assistance.

However, a few moments later, my thoughts shifted: *"How exactly . . . am I supposed to use a secretary?"* Until this point, I had never been in charge of other adults, and I certainly had never been taught how to manage the roles and responsibilities of this position.

Little did I know my relationship with my secretary would be one of the most important—and most complicated—relationships as a school leader.

■ ■ ■

The more I work with other school leaders, the more I realize relationships with secretaries (also referred to as assistants or administrative assistants) are far from perfect.

Leaders who assume new positions rely heavily on their secretaries. Not only do they know everything about the building, secretaries also control many of the organization's logistical and communicative processes. So, when leaders have questions about building operations, secretaries are the first place they turn.

In most cases, these relationships start great. Eager to make the relationship work—and weary of making changes—administrators defer many decisions to secretaries. Even if they don't necessarily agree with or understand certain processes, administrators are willing to follow past practice.

However, as administrators learn the lay of the land, their reliance on secretaries lessens. Whereas initially they may have asked their secretary for advice, over time leaders become comfortable making their own decisions and pushing personal priorities.

This relational shift can get quite tricky. Many incumbent secretaries have been in their roles for years and are used to doing things a certain way. So, when the new leader wants to make changes, some secretaries resist the change. *"We've done it this way for the last five principals . . . why should I change now?"*

If this scenario resonates with you, take comfort in knowing you are not alone. I have experienced this resistance to change with several secretaries. And to be honest, it's hard to blame them!

Many secretaries work for numerous leaders. With administrator turnover reaching all-time highs, lifelong secretaries could work for *double-digit* bosses over the course of a career. Even the most adaptable assistants become weary of bosses who insist, *"We need to make changes"* when they are likely to leave in the next couple years.

■ ■ ■

How do administrators create a relationship where secretaries feel empowered and valued, while still understanding that their main purpose is to support the leader? Here are seven ideas:

Weekly Meetings: Many readers will say, *"I meet with my secretary all the time, I don't need a weekly meeting."* Unfortunately, these conversations usually focus on the leader's needs—not the secretary's needs. Leaders should schedule weekly 1:1 meetings (at least 30 minutes in length) where the goal of these conversations is for secretaries to discuss the topics that are most important to them.

Set Expectations: The first weeks on the job are vital for school leaders to establish expectations with employees, and secretaries are no different. Leaders must take advantage of these early conversations to create boundaries for the relationship. Leaders would be wise to say something along the lines of:

> *I'm excited to use these first several months to learn from you and the processes that you already have in place. But please understand that I bring a unique perspective to this position and will likely make changes at some point.*

No Surprises: School leaders are often guilty of keeping secretaries in the dark on important decisions. *"They don't need to know everything that goes on,"* these leaders explain. Unfortunately, this archaic way of thinking does not serve leaders well in a time when information travels at record speeds. Not only does sharing important information with secretaries build the relationship, it also prepares the secretary when complaints funnel through the office.

ERA and Career Goals: In *Permission to be Great,* Dan Butler discusses "ERA" which is an acronym for *encouragement, recognition,* and *appreciation.*[22] It is *vital* that school leaders positively reinforce their secretaries for the purpose of engagement and retention. Furthermore, leaders should initiate conversations about professional goals, helping to carve out pathways for secretaries who are looking to advance their careers.

Flexibility: Unlike teachers and classroom paras who are expected to be in front of kids 90% of the day, secretaries have more flexibility in their jobs. Employees crave autonomy, and bosses should be flexible in how they treat secretarial hours. Office staff should never feel bad about leaving for an appointment, taking a long lunch, or working from home while tending to a sick child. While some traditional secretaries may not care, most secretaries value a flexible work environment.

Coaching: Let's be honest, not every secretary is a rock star. Some mediocre secretaries are passed down from leader to leader without any coaching. Similar to how teachers must be given training to improve deficiencies, secretaries must be provided with opportunities to improve. Whether the shortcomings are technology related (quite often) or customer-service related (more difficult to address), school leaders must communicate these issues and develop plans for improvement.

Make a Change: What if you have done everything listed and still don't feel like you are getting the most out of your secretary? It may be time to make a change. *"But they know so much about our building,"* some leaders argue. *"How will we replace them?"* While initially there may be a steep learning curve (see what I did there?), leaders who find a secretary who is open to new ideas and hungry for the opportunity find that changing personnel can make a world of difference.

■ ■ ■

As I look back on my first years in administration, I realize I had *no clue* how to properly utilize a secretary. Heck—15 years in educational leadership—and I still have plenty to learn about this partnership.

If you find yourself wondering why the relationship between boss and secretary is such hard work, understand the following:

It's complicated.

THE 3% RULE

Walk into any bookstore and you'll find countless personal finance books promoting specialized budgets. In these texts, authors provide step-by-step plans for monthly income allocations.

For example, in *All Your Worth: The Ultimate Lifetime Money Plan*, Elizabeth Warren and Amelia Warren Tyagi propose the 50/30/20 Budget. This plan suggests that income should be split three ways: 50% on needs, 30% on wants, and 20% on savings.[23]

Best-selling author Dave Ramsey also provides percentage guidelines. In *The Total Money Makeover*, Ramsey proposes that readers separate their budgets across 11 areas, with housing (25%), food (10% to 15%), insurance (10% to 25%), and transportation (10%) being notable areas.[24]

Other prominent budgeting plans include the pay-yourself-first budget (address savings and debt first and then spend the rest), the envelope system budget (establish a cash limit for each spending category), and the zero-based budget (income minus expenses equals zero).

I'd like to present a different type of budgeting plan—a plan that is unlike any other. This budgeting plan:

Only has one category.
Only applies to school leaders.
Only appears in this book.

This budgeting plan is called: *The 3% Rule.*

The 3% Rule reads as follows: *"When educators accept an administrative position, they must assume that 3% of their salary will go back to the school or district in which they work."*

For example, principals with a $100,000 salary should expect that $3,000 will go back to their school in the form of donations, fundraisers, gifts, and other work-related expenses. The same ratio can be used for assistant principals ($80,000 = $2,400), superintendents ($150,000 = $4,500), and administrators at all levels.

"Three thousand dollars?" you may be thinking. *"That's a lot of money!"*

Unfortunately, this mentality hurts the perception of school administrators. Even though they make three, four, and even *five times* as much as their employees, school leaders have earned a reputation for being cheap when it comes to opening their personal pocketbooks.

Whether or not this perception is accurate is irrelevant. What matters is when they are elevated to the administrative level, school leaders must understand that their spending habits will suddenly be placed under the public microscope.

■ ■ ■

Like many educators, I grew up in a middle-class family. While we always had food on the table and a roof over our heads, by no means did we live a life of luxury.

Typical of many 1980s families, my dad worked full time while my mom stayed at home to take care of my three siblings and me. Given the fact that six people were living off of my dad's modest salary, we got used to living on a tight budget.

In our house, "special occasion" meant going to McDonalds, "new clothes" meant getting hand-me-downs, and "family vacation" meant a trip to Adventureland in Des Moines.

Despite living on a tight budget, you know we had to get them black Nikes.

After my parents separated when I was in fifth grade, things got especially tight. Suddenly my mom was waiting on tables at Applebee's to make ends meet. Even though my dad paid child support, my siblings and I found ourselves eating free lunches at school and receiving other forms of financial assistance.

I can vividly remember going to one of my affluent friend's houses one day after school. When we opened the kitchen cabinets, I was shocked by the snack food selection: Gushers, DunkAroos, Handi-Snacks, Pop Tarts . . . our options were endless!

Noticing my surprise, my buddy asked me what I normally ate after school. Recalling a recent conversation with my mom, I explained that we were often told to *go out back and pick an apple off the tree* (true story—ask my siblings).

When I went to college, it was more of the same. Whereas most peers received financial assistance from parents, it was understood that scholarships, loans, and getting a job would be my source of income. Being a broke college student meant you learned how to mooch off others and how to cut your own hair (would not recommend).

These booklets were my best friend from 2000 to 2004.

Whereas I will forever be appreciative of my humble upbringing, one side effect of being raised in a working-class family was that I was trained to always look for ways to save money. Even when I started to make the "big bucks" as a school administrator, this frugal mindset persisted.

For example, as a young assistant principal, students would often try to sell me T-shirts or cookie dough as part of a school fundraiser. Programmed by my parents to never spend money on frivolous items, my natural reaction was to tell kids *"come back later"* with hopes that they would never return.

Another example was employee gifts. Growing up, I was taught to spend as little as possible on presents. Rather than buy expensive gifts for friends and family, we learned how to make gifts for others because—in the end—it was the "thought that counts."

So, when it dawned on me that I was expected to buy my secretary a birthday gift, my thriftiness kicked in. Whereas I should have been excited about doing something nice for my assistant, instead I was more concerned with limiting the cost of the gift.

However, six years into school administration I experienced a turning point in my spending philosophy. In *Learning Curve*, I shared how one administrative team I worked with was so cheap that we decided against buying individual holiday gifts for office staff. Instead, we used the district credit card to purchase juice and donuts.

"We make so much more than our secretaries," I thought to myself. *"Couldn't we have done something a little more thoughtful?"* Embarrassed by my actions and general attitude toward spending, I vowed to stop being so cheap from that point forward.

Almost immediately, I began looking for opportunities to give back to our school in the form of donations, fundraisers, and gifts. Rather than worry about the money spent, I began to treat each purchase as an opportunity to build strong relationships and improve organizational culture.

I found these moments to be hugely gratifying. Whereas buying things for myself initially made me happy, these moments were short-lived. On the other hand, giving back to students and employees produced moments of prolonged joy.

One story that illustrates this thinking occurred in April of 2020. It was at this time I heard that one of our paraeducators and her husband were both struggling with COVID. Figuring they could use some help, I sent the family a check for $50 along with a handwritten get-well card.

A few weeks later, the employee visited the district office to drop off medical paperwork. When finished, she popped her head into my office and told me how thankful she was for the gift. *"We used your money to buy Casey's pizza for dinner,"* she told me. *"We hadn't been able to do that for a long time. Our kids were so happy!"*

Not only did I build a close bond with the employee, I feel good every time I recall the story. Research supports the positive effects of giving. In *Happy Money*, Elizabeth Dunn and Michael Norton report:

> *Spending even small amounts of money on others can make a difference for our own happiness. Studies have shown that individuals who spend money on others are measurably happier than those who spend money on themselves. The more people spend on others, the happier they feel.*[25]

I encourage you to actively notice your levels of happiness when you make certain purchases. Whereas buying a new Patagonia jacket or lululemon leggings could provide initial bursts of happiness, those feelings are likely short-lived compared to the happiness felt if the next time a student offers you a World's Finest Chocolate candy bar you say, *"I'll buy the whole box."*

■ ■ ■

Curious as to where 3% of a school administrator's salary might go? Assuming a $100,000 salary, here is a possible breakdown:

Gifts ($1,000): Gift giving should be viewed as a small—*yet potent*—type of ammo in the leader's employee appreciation arsenal. Leaders should get in the habit of giving *every* direct report—not just their assistant—generous gifts for birthdays and the holidays. Furthermore, thoughtful bosses who purchase tokens of appreciation matching employee interest areas can take relationships to extraordinary levels.

Organizations ($500): Booster clubs, parent-teacher associations, scholarship committees, alumni organizations . . . schools are full of these groups. School leaders should contribute to these clubs on an annual basis. Given that influential parents and community members run these groups, administrators should view these as high-leverage giving opportunities.

Fundraisers ($500): Schools are full of fundraisers throughout the year. When kids (and parents) approach them with requests, school leaders must be willing to open their pocketbooks and make purchases even if they don't really need chocolate-covered peanuts or another magazine subscription.

Donations ($500): There are times throughout the year when donations to different causes are needed. For example, families often collect money for students who are battling cancer or recovering from traumatic injuries. Leaders who give to these causes not only feel a sense of fulfillment, they build lifelong bonds with those families.

Other ($500): Mileage, parking, meals, snacks, flowers . . . over the course of the year, school leaders accumulate a number of costs in which they must ask themselves: *"Do I ask for reimbursement or do I take the hit?"* Rather than nickel and dime the district for every expense—which makes them look cheap—leaders must strategically select times for reimbursement.

You jelly? Hundreds of dollars have been spent giving away free donuts.

■ ■ ■

John F. Kennedy famously said, *"For of those to whom much is given, much is required."* [26]

School leaders—stop being so cheap.

Rather than overthink every expenditure, assume that 3% of your salary will go back to your school district.

Entry Plan Template

When interviewing for principal and superintendent openings, candidates are often asked to bring an entry plan to share with the interview committee.

Entry plans give school leaders a chance to share their goals and aspirations for the first year on the job. While entry plans aren't the most enjoyable to create, they are a valuable practice because they force a school leader to hone in on their top priorities during the leadership transition.

I have interviewed for several school leadership positions over the past 15 years. Although these interviews have been the source of great frustration, one silver lining is that I've had plenty of practice in creating interview documents such as cover letters, resumes, and entry plans.

The following is the entry plan that was used when I was named Superintendent of the Waterloo (Iowa) Community School District. This plan caught the eye of many in the leadership community, and is now used as an "exemplar" in many educational leadership programs.

Feel free to use my plan as a template for creating your own document.

■ ■ ■

Preentry: Connections & Logistics (March—June)

*"Two things remain irretrievable:
time and a first impression"*

—CYNTHIA OZICK

Prior to my official start date with Waterloo Community School District, I plan to meet with direct reports, district administrators, and other district leadership team members. Meetings will include 1:1 and group meetings. The purpose of these conversations is to **build relationships with employees, learn more about the Waterloo schools,** and **collaborate on important decisions** prior to July 1st.

Next, I will make myself readily available to school board members and all Waterloo employees for the purpose of **establishing connections** as well as **staying up to speed on changing developments** in the weeks leading up to my formal assumption of the role. Other action steps include: attending school board meetings, researching the district, engaging with the community on social media, conversations with stakeholders, taking part in virtual meetings, and helping transition my current district.

Finally, I will spend plenty of time with Pam Arndorfer to **build our relationship,** share our various experiences and perspectives for working together, and to draft a schedule for the coming months.

Phase 1: Relationship Building (July—August)

*"The most important ingredient of success is
knowing how to get along with people."*

—THEODORE ROOSEVELT

The initial entry into the district presents an important opportunity to establish relationships throughout the community and **establish a tone of approachability, openness, and positivity.** Therefore, my top priority during these first six weeks will be to generate opportunities to meet and interact with a wide variety of district employees, community members, and district stakeholders.

The purpose of my conversations will be to **understand each individual's unique perspective on the school district** as well as **explore his or her vision for the future of the Waterloo Community Schools.** To help guide our conversations, I will ask the three questions listed below.

1. What should the Waterloo Schools keep doing?
2. What should the Waterloo Schools stop doing?
3. What should the Waterloo Schools start doing?

Starting in July and culminating by the end of the 2022 calendar year, my goal is to **make personal, in-person contact with all 1,400 Waterloo School District employees.** This will be done through a combination of focus groups as well as formal and informal visits. The key themes and patterns that emerge during those conversations will help guide our district vision work in the years ahead.

Furthermore, I will implement a practice I started four years ago which is to **send every Waterloo student a personal, handwritten**

postcard on his or her birthday. While this will take time and resources, I have found this to be one of my most impactful practices as a school superintendent.

Finally, I will continue to seek out conversations with various stakeholder groups, such as current students, recent graduates, parent groups, the Waterloo Educators Association and other bargaining groups, community political leaders, major employers, small business owners, church leaders, and nonprofit organizations. In addition to **crafting the future district vision**, these conversations will **reinforce a culture of collaboration and trust between the community and school district.**

Phase 2: Seeking to Understand (August—September)

"Seek first to understand, then to be understood."

—STEVEN COVEY

First, I will meet with key personnel for the purpose of understanding our instructional supports. Areas include curriculum and instruction, special and gifted education, equity and inclusion, alternative education, and other specialty programs. These conversations will analyze district student performance data, with specific attention focused on **achievement gaps in terms of minority and economically disadvantaged students.** Finally, we will discuss how at-risk supports such as counseling, school-based mental health, family-community liaisons, and health-care providers help us reach our goals.

Second, I will meet with leaders and key personnel in human resources, finances, transportation, maintenance, and food service. Furthermore, I will **prioritize meeting with, observing, and understanding the work of support staff.** Not only will this help foster relationships with a large percentage of Waterloo staff, I will also develop an understanding and appreciation of their work.

Finally, as the end of summer nears I will deliver a welcome and charge to the staff to kick off the school year. The goal of the presentation will be twofold: to be **lighthearted and vulnerable for the purpose of building trust** while also establishing that we are an organization where **every employee matters** and **plays a role in our success.** Finally, during the first week of school I will **spend time in every Waterloo building** welcoming staff, engaging with students, and introducing myself to parents.

Phase 3: Setting the Course (September—November)

"Life's a marathon, not a sprint."

—Phillip C. McGraw

Phase 3 will be more of the same as I continue to visit buildings, engage with students, and speak with employees. Understanding the wishes and dreams of a school district cannot be forced, meaning stakeholders must feel like **their voices are heard and that they have opportunities to provide feedback.** Therefore, determining the right path of action for the Waterloo Schools will take a full school year. My goal is to deliver a renewed vision for the Waterloo Schools to start the 2023–2024 school year.

Please note that **I do not plan to make any large, systemic changes during the first year.** Too many leaders begin a job feeling compelled to make sweeping changes for the purpose of displaying their aptitude and "making their mark." I have learned—through my own mistakes—that effective leaders must **take time to listen and to honor the work that is already being done.** Unless there is overwhelming consensus that drastic change needs to occur, **my first year will focus on listening and understanding.**

Phase 4: Delivery (December—Beyond)

"The journey is the lives we touch, the legacy we leave, and the world we change for the better."

—Tony Dungy

This entry plan starts with building strong relationships and culminates with a renewed vision for the district. But while this plan details an initial flurry of activity, **building relationships, trust, and vision is a never-ending process.** The transformation of any aspiration into reality requires an alignment of project planning, timing, budgeting, execution, progress monitoring, and accountability.

Throughout all four phases of my entry **I will utilize traditional and social media to share my journey of engagement** with the community. Not only will this approach reinforce my goal of creating a tone of openness and availability, it will also provide more opportunities to engage with stakeholders.

I am excited about the possibility of leading this effort with the Waterloo Community Schools. The district has a rich tradition, and I believe it is capable of being recognized as **the standard for** urban education in the state of Iowa. Together, we will deliver greatness for the children of Waterloo.

■ ■ ■

Before we leave this chapter, I want to be clear that an entry plan should be a work in progress. Just because an entry plan worked for one district does not mean that the entry plan will work for the next district.

I cringe when I see school leaders recycle old entry plans, changing only the name of the school or the district at the top. Not only does this show a lack of motivation for the job, people who copy and paste interview materials miss out on valuable opportunities to learn about the district.

Remember: the best leaders are *lifelong learners*. People who are passionate about self-improvement look at previous entry plans and think, *"Wow—I could have made that a whole lot better!"*

Author Alain de Botton said it best: *"Anyone who isn't embarrassed of who they were last year probably isn't learning enough."*

Recommended Reading: Leadership

In addition to the books already referenced in *Turning Points*, below are fifteen more *leadership* titles to add to your reading list. While not exhaustive, these resources provide a good starting point for anyone wanting to dig deeper into the leadership philosophies shared in these pages.

Books are arranged alphabetically by author.

‣ *Lead from the Outside,* by Stacey Abrams

‣ *Daring Greatly,* by Brene Brown

‣ *How to Win Friends and Influence People,* by Dale Carnegie

‣ *It's the Manager,* by Jim Clifton and Jim Harter

‣ *The Culture Code Playbook,* by Daniel Coyle

‣ *Principles,* by Ray Dalio

‣ *Quiet Strength,* by Tony Dungy

‣ *Can't Hurt Me,* by David Goggins

‣ *The Power of Positive Leadership,* by Jon Gordon

‣ *Rework, by* David Heinemeier Hansson and Jason Fried

‣ *The Leadership Challenge,* by James Kouzes and Barry Posner

‣ *The Five Dysfunctions of a Team,* by Patrick Lencioni

‣ *So Good They Can't Ignore You,* by Cal Newport

‣ *Radical Candor,* by Kim Scott

‣ *Never Split the Difference,* by Chris Voss

For more book ideas, visit: *www.drjaredsmith.com/book-summaries*

EDUCATION

"The only real mistake is the one from which we learn nothing."

—HENRY FORD

ADDRESSING THE TEACHER SHORTAGE

When asked to share the biggest challenge facing today's schools, one answer has risen to the top for school leaders: *the teacher shortage.*

Certainly, there is truth to these claims. According to the *Learning Policy Institute*, schools in the United States were short more than 100,000 teachers in 2020 . . . *before* the COVID pandemic.[1] And as the number of teachers exiting the profession *doubles* the number of students entering teacher preparation programs, these numbers figure to get much worse.

As is the case with any dilemma, school leaders have two options: *complain about the problem* or *figure out solutions.*

Those who complain about the teacher shortage say:

"Politicians need to give schools more money!"
"Colleges need to attract more students to the field!"
"Society needs to stop being so hard on educators!"

Those who look for solutions to the teacher shortage say:

"How can we attract more teachers?"
"How can we improve our hiring processes?"
"How can we keep teachers from leaving?"

Consider the phrases used in your district.

Are you spending your time blaming others?
Or, are you actively searching for solutions?

■ ■ ■

On Episode #98 of *The Group Project Podcast*, I interviewed Roark Horn, who served as the Executive Director of School Administrators of Iowa. During our interview, I asked Roark, *"What advice do you have for school leaders who are dealing with a teacher shortage?"*

Here was his response:

> *Simply put, I would make your district a destination district. We're going to be in competition for teachers early in their career. When you are in competition, you want to put your best foot forward. What are you doing as a district to prepare yourself for this possibility so that you are attractive to people?*

Many schools place teacher recruitment low on their priority list. Instead of strategizing how to attract highly talented employees, leaders prioritize test scores, instructional frameworks, student behaviors, social-emotional learning, professional-learning communities, and other initiatives.

While all are important for school success, the previous statement poses a subtle irony: when schools recruit, hire, and retain effective staff, *initiatives have a way of taking care of themselves.*

■ ■ ■

A short time ago, I was in one of our buildings and saw a familiar face chatting with the principal.

"Do you remember me?" this individual asked.

"Yes, of course I do!" I responded. *"You used to sub for us. How are things going?"*

"Well, that's why I'm here. I took a full-time job (in a nearby district). Honestly, I don't like it there. I don't feel valued, and my opinion doesn't seem to matter.

"You guys were different," she continued. *"You spent time getting to know me. And I was just a sub! It felt special working here. Everyone was so friendly and welcoming.*

"I want to come back."

The principal and I exchanged big grins. Not only did it feel good to hear how much of an impact our culture made on this person, it's not every day you have a teacher begging to work for you.

This speaks to the notion that today's leaders must possess a *recruitment mentality.* Rather than search for staff only when they have openings, administrators must actively recruit staff *at all times.*

How much time do you invest in subs, student teachers, and practicum students? Whereas some leaders say, *"I don't have the time!",*" forward-thinking administrators view these individuals as prime candidates to fill vacant positions.

The same could be said for interactions outside of work. School leaders who want to keep their buildings fully staffed must approach *every* interaction through a recruitment lens, understanding that you never know where you'll find your next employee.

One of my favorite stories to tell is how I found a rockstar custodian at a Casey's convenience store. One winter morning, I was waiting in line to pay for a Peach Mango Bang when a voice behind me said, *"Are you Dr. Smith?"*

If you know, you know.

I turned around and saw a middle-aged man who I had never seen before. He said he knew me from social media and had heard good things about my leadership. During our discussion, he shared that he was unhappy in his current job, and was looking at other options. Immediately, I went into recruitment mode and asked to exchange numbers so we could stay in touch.

A few weeks later, I texted him about a custodian opening in one of our buildings. Beyond simply alerting him of the position, I sent him the link to the online posting, passed along his name to our building principal, and told our HR department to be on the lookout for his application. Essentially, my goal was to remove all barriers that would prevent this individual from being hired.

Two weeks later, he was introduced as our new custodian.

Whether it's the hard-working gentleman who stocks shelves at the grocery store, or the pleasant secretary who works at city hall, school leaders must always be on the lookout for talented individuals who could potentially fill workplace vacancies.

■ ■ ■

Looking for more ideas about teacher recruitment and retainment? Here are seven suggestions:

Post Jobs Early: Starting the hiring process early is vital as school districts battle over a dwindling number of qualified applicants. To get an accurate picture of the openings they will have the following year, schools should issue contracts as early as possible (in Iowa this day is March 15th). While they may not be legally binding, contracts are a major piece of the hiring puzzle that should be finalized ASAP.

Market Job Openings: Many school districts use outdated approaches to promote teacher openings. Rather than passively posting openings on job search websites and in local newspapers, school leaders must proactively market vacancies using social media and other forms of digital communication. In a time when teachers are in high demand, districts must ensure openings are seen by large audiences.

Be Aggressive: If you have ever been heavily recruited for a job, you realize how good it feels to be wanted. Turn on the charm and persuade candidates as to why they are needed in your building.

Furthermore, consider sending "cold" emails, texts, and Facebook messages to potential candidates. I have sent hundreds of "Hail Mary" messages over the years, and—while only 10 or so have panned out—those are 10 positions that likely would have gone unfilled had I not been persistent in finding candidates.

SOUTH TAMA COUNTY PARA OPENINGS

As of June 14th, 2021

2 Elementary Paras
2 Elementary Special Ed Paras
1 Middle School Special Ed Para
1 High School Special Ed Para
1 Alternative School Para

$13-$15/HOUR STARTING PAY
HEALTH BENEFITS FOR SOME POSITIONS
ALL POSITIONS INCLUDE "IPERS" PAY
WORK WITH STUDENTS IN A FRIENDLY,
POSITIVE ENVIRONMENT!

This particular post was shared more than 50 times and seen by thousands of people on Facebook.

Employee Referral Bonus: Do not underestimate word-of-mouth marketing when it comes to teacher recruitment. Research shows that 92% of people trust recommendations from friends and family more than traditional advertising.[2] By offering a referral bonus to current staff who recruit new teachers to the district (we offer $250 for each new hire), employees are encouraged to contact friends when jobs become available.

Our employees love when we surprise them with one of our oversized checks!

Empower Administrators: One of the biggest misconceptions in school leadership is that Human Resources is the only department that can discuss salaries with potential employees. Not only is this untrue, this practice creates massive organizational bottlenecks . . . slowing down the hiring process when time is of the essence. As long as they avoid promising candidates a precise income, leaders should not only be trusted to discuss salaries, but also they should be empowered to *negotiate salaries* using a set of clear guidelines.

Employee Check-In: Administrators who are committed to keeping their buildings fully staffed must engage employees in retention-focused conversations. *"Are you happy in your current role?," "Do you plan to return next year?,"* and *"Are you looking at other jobs?"* are reasonable questions to ask. Leaders who take time to understand where each employee stands are rarely caught off guard by a surprise resignation.

Stay Interviews: We've all heard of *exit* interviews. But what about *stay* interviews? Rather than reactively ask employees why they are leaving, leaders should proactively ask employees what makes them stick around. *"What motivates you to work in our school?"*, *"What could be better about your work experience?"*, and *"What opportunities within our district do you want to pursue?"* are questions that can take retention-focused conversations to the next level.

■ ■ ■

One topic that deserves its own section is employee compensation.

When school leaders propose teacher retainment solutions, the most common answer is to increase employee compensation. *"We just need to pay our teachers more money!"* administrators say, assuming compensation is the magic bullet. With this in mind, schools across the country are announcing long-term raises and one-time bonuses for staff.

Obviously, teacher compensation is a major concern and school leaders must continue pushing educator salaries higher to ensure they are competitive with other professions.

However—when you examine the root cause of job dissatisfaction—compensation is rarely the primary factor. In a recent study examining the most common reasons employees leave a position, only 12% of employees cited *"wanting more money"* as the primary cause for leaving a job.[3]

Rather than compensation, employees cited *lack of flexibility, unempathetic bosses, team tension, lack of engagement, lack of appreciation,* and *lack of opportunities* as bigger factors when leaving a position.

"Yeah, but schools are different," some readers may be thinking. *"When the district next door pays more money, employees will leave!"*

In *It's the Manager: Moving from Boss to Coach,* Jim Clifton and Jim Harter explain that across all job professions, it takes a 20% pay increase for employees to leave jobs they love.[4] Alternately, it takes a 0% pay increase for employees to leave jobs they hate. This means that a teacher making $50,000 would need to make $60,000 in another district to consider quitting.

Think about how your district salary structure compares to those around you. Certainly, if you are paying teachers 20% less than the neighboring district, it's hard to blame teachers for leaving. However, my experience is that teacher compensation is fairly consistent across districts . . . meaning that money is rarely the deciding factor when employees choose to leave.

The lesson here is when employees feel valued, they rarely leave a position just to make a little more money at the neighboring district.

■ ■ ■

Listen, folks: *the teacher shortage isn't going away any time soon.* In fact, it's going to get much, much worse.

What is your response?

Are you going to sulk and blame others about the situation? Or, are you going to create your own destination district?

It's TIME to Address Teacher Burnout

As districts continue to adjust to life in a postpandemic world, *teacher burnout* has become a hot topic of conversation.

Consider all that is being asked of teachers. Not only was teaching an incredibly demanding job *before* the pandemic . . . now we are asking teachers to make up a year's worth of learning loss, deal with a spike in student social emotional issues, and—thanks to a nationwide sub shortage—cover more classrooms than ever before.

It's no wonder teachers are leaving the profession in droves.

Unfortunately, some districts continue to march forward with strategic plans and new initiatives as if burnout is nonexistent. *"We've got to get our kids caught up"* leaders justify upon adding another task to teachers' already-full plates.

But say you want to address teacher burnout. What practical steps can schools implement to address this important issue?

Better pay?
Improved benefits?
Self-care training?

Social gatherings?

Free yoga classes?

Bring puppies to work?

While I have tried every one of these ideas (yes, even bringing puppies to work), one gift stands alone when addressing educator fatigue: *the gift of time.*

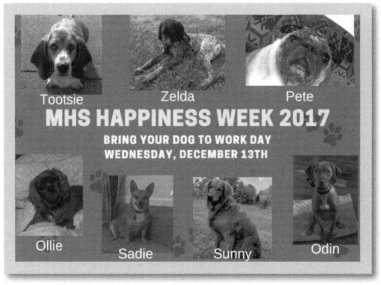

"Bring Your Dog to Work Day" was one of my favorite traditions as a building principal!

■ ■ ■

Certainly, we could theorize the *gift of time* is important to staff. But what does the research say?

Gary Chapman is best known for his research on romantic relationships. In 1992, he published *The 5 Love Languages* which explored how couples express and receive love.[5] Chapman found when couples invest time to learn their partner's five unique styles of communicating love—*the five love languages*—they build stronger and longer-lasting relationships.

Given the enormous success of the Love Languages research, Chapman teamed with Paul White to discover the keys to effective relationships at work. Called *The Five Languages of Appreciation in the Workplace*, the authors sought to help supervisors effectively communicate appreciation to their employees, which would result in greater job satisfaction, healthier relationships . . . and decreased burnout.[6]

Among their key findings, Chapman and White discovered that *time* has become the most valued commodity for employees: "*For a while, 'time off' was seen as something that the younger employees primarily wanted. But we have found that 'time' has become the most valued resource for most employees, regardless of age group.*"

Unfortunately, the educational system does the exact opposite of the research. Rather than trust staff to manage their time, school administrators are notorious for micromanaging employees. Eight-hour workdays, canned curriculum, thirty-minute lunches, structured planning periods . . . schools are the *antithesis* of workplace autonomy.

Now when it comes to "time off," schools are admittedly limited in the amount of vacation time they can offer employees. Given that 90% of an educators' day consists of actively engaging with children, teachers can't exactly come and go as they please.

However, school leaders must understand the psychological importance of time. Rather than throw their hands up and say, "*We run a school, there is nothing we can do!*" school leaders must get creative in how they manage the workday.

■ ■ ■

One of my favorite professional practices is to complete 20-minute "rounding" meetings with teachers (see page 19). The purpose of these conversations is to create a safe space for sharing honest feedback, while also getting to know staff on a personal level.

In 2021—the first "normal" year after the pandemic—I began rounding meetings in September. Since school had just started, I assumed most teachers were still in the "honeymoon" period to begin the year. Unfortunately, the exact opposite was true. Not only were teachers reporting high levels of stress and fatigue, "burnout" was a common theme across my conversations.

The following are notes from a meeting with a middle school teacher dated September 20th:

> *This year we are dealing with less COVID issues, but we are still coping with the stress. The kids are tough . . . and I'm being asked to cover classes . . . I just give so much of myself each day. There are days when I go home and just sit down because I'm exhausted. I don't know what it is, but I feel more tired and stressed than ever before.*

Here are notes from a conversation with a high school teacher dated September 23rd:

> *This is my 16th year as a teacher. It's also been my most difficult. I feel as stressed as I would in December, and we're only five weeks into school. I am stressed beyond belief. The constant covering . . . it's really taking a toll. We need time. We need more time.*

Regardless of building level or content area, the themes of stress, exhaustion, and fatigue kept popping up in our conversations.

Realizing we needed to quickly come up with a plan or risk losing staff (both figuratively and literally), a colleague and I brainstormed ideas that would show staff *"We hear you."*

We discussed several ideas: offer mindfulness training, hand-deliver goodie bags, take staff to a movie, bring in food trucks for lunch. But when the dust settled, one thought rose above the rest: *giving teachers time.*

We generated a plan that would add one two-hour early dismissal each month for the rest of the school year. By having students leave early, teachers would gain much-needed planning time. To be clear, this was not "additional" planning time . . . but rather, planning time we owed teachers who were constantly being asked to cover empty classrooms.

When we presented this idea during an all-staff meeting, our teachers were thrilled. Not only did they desperately need the planning time, they were ecstatic that we had listened and were honoring their feedback. And after reviewing a survey in which 90% of employees favored the plan, it became clear that *time* is what staff wanted.

One small hurdle existed: school board approval. Given this plan would change the school calendar, we needed the school board's blessing on the idea. Nevertheless, after explaining the thought process, sharing the survey data, and providing answers to potential pitfalls (more on this to come), the school board unanimously approved our recommendation.

Dr. Jared Smith
@JaredSmithPhD   ...

UPDATE: Due to a sub shortage, STC teachers gave up 200-plus hours of planning during the first month of school.

To offset this loss (and future losses), STC has announced three additional 1:15pm early dismissals for 1st semester: 10/22, 11/12, and 12/10

More info to come!! 🩶 🖤

2021-2022 STC School Calendar	August 2021					Student Days/Hours		180 Days/1080 Hours Calendar

2021-2022
STC School Calendar

Summary of Calendar
Student Days/Hours in Classroom:
First Semester............81 / 499.5
Second Semester......98 / 613
TOTAL DAYS/HRS   179 / 1112.5

CALENDAR LEGEND

Parent Teacher Conferences

Prof. Dev.
No School

Early Out

Conf. Comp Day
No School

End of Quarter

August 2021

M	T	W	Th	F	Student Days/Hours	
16	17	18	19	20	0	0
23	24	25	26	27	5	30.5
30	31				2	13

September 2021

	1	2	3	3	18.5
6	7	8	9	10	4	25
13	14	15	16	17	5	31.5
20	21	22	23	24	5	31.5
27	28	29	30		4	25

October 2021

				1	0	0
4	5	6	7	8	5	31.5
11	12	13	14	15	5	31.5
18	19	20	21	22	5	29.5
25	26	27	28		4	24

November 2021

1	2	3	4	5	5	31.5
8	9	10	11	12	5	29.5
15	16	17	18	19	5	31.5
22	23	24	25	26	2	13
29	30				2	13

December 2021

		1	2	3	3	18.5
6	7	8	9	10	5	29.5
13	14	15	16	17	5	31.5
20	21	22	23	24	2	11
27	28	29	30	31	0	0

180 Days/1080 Hours Calendar

Aug. 17, 18, 19, 20	Prof. Dev. (No School)
Aug. 23	First Day for Students (K-12)
	Early Out (1 Hour)
Aug. 25	Early Out (1 hour)
Sept. 1	Early Out (1 hour)
Sept. 2	First Day for Preschool
Sept. 6	Labor Day (No School)
Sept. 8, 15, 22, 29	Early Out (1 hour)
Oct. 1	Prof. Dev. (No School)
Oct. 6, 13	Early Out (1 hour)
Oct. 18	End of 1st Qt (39 days)
Oct. 20	Early Out (1 hour)
Oct. 22	Early Out (2 hours)
Oct. 26, 28	Parent Teacher Conference (Early Out - 1 Hour)
Oct. 29	Comp Day (No School)
Nov. 3, 10	Early Out (1 hour)
Nov. 12	Early Out (2 hours)
Nov. 17	Early Out (1 hour)
Nov. 24, 25, 26	Holiday Break (No School)
Dec. 1, 8	Early Out (1 hour)
Dec. 10	Early Out (2 hours)
Dec. 15	Early Out (1 hour)
Dec. 21	End of 2nd Qt (42 days)
Dec. 22 - 31	Holiday Break (No School)

2:45 PM · Oct 7, 2021 · Twitter Web App

ılı View Tweet activity

57 Retweets   **39** Quote Tweets   **358** Likes

Our decision to give teachers additional planning time garnered lots of attention on social media.

▪ ▪ ▪

When others heard about our plan, several questions emerged. The following were my responses to the most common queries:

"What about student supervision?" Student supervision must be discussed any time a school considers adjusting the daily schedule. Assuming that leaving work was not an option for most parents, we arranged for paras to supervise students. We also asked our transportation department to run two separate bus routes: one at the early dismissal time (1:15pm) and one at the regular dismissal time (3:15pm).

"What about lost instructional time?" Philosophically, this was the most difficult question. The pandemic caused a year's worth of learning loss . . . so how could we justify giving up more instructional time? However, one could argue that whatever instructional time had been lost would be regained— *and even exceeded*—when teachers were better prepared to teach the material and more motivated to perform their jobs at high levels.

"Will your staff abuse the time?" One more time for the people in the back: *leaders must make decisions based on their best staff.* Unfortunately, too many administrators worry about their worst staff and make decisions for all based on the poor decisions of a few. This mindset results in schools never pushing forward with new innovations. Finally, if you have staff who you know will abuse time . . . *why are they still in your organization?*

"Won't your community complain?" Every community has individuals who complain about school decisions. While these people can be exhausting, understand that community perception impacts the leader's influence. Rather than ignore the obvious

obstacles of a decision, administrators should forecast potential questions and address those concerns when an announcement is made.

> Leaders must empower employees to make decisions on their own.
>
> If the organization is full of people whom nobody trusts to make decisions, then the organization is full of the wrong people.
>
> #TurningPoints

"But it's hard to collect data!" It's crazy to see how many districts make subjective decisions rather than collect objective data. Leaders must search for multiple data points to help justify difficult decisions. *"Yeah, but our staff hates surveys,"* you may be thinking. The reason most staff don't like surveys is because leadership never uses their feedback!

"Cool plan! But it won't work here." Why do so many school leaders lack the initiative to implement good ideas? *It's hard work.* The process of scheduling rounding meetings, encouraging critical feedback, brainstorming possible solutions, generating employee buy-in, and implementing change takes time and energy. But isn't that what leaders are paid the "big bucks" to do?

■ ■ ■

Teacher burnout isn't going away.

In fact, it's only going to get worse.

While several options could help teachers, one solution rises above the rest: *The gift of time.*

First Impressions Matter

In *The Power of Moments*, Chip and Dan Heath share the following:

> *The lack of attention paid to an employee's first day is mind-boggling. What a wasted opportunity to make a new team member feel included and appreciated. To avoid this kind of oversight, we must understand when special moments are needed . . . to spot the occasions that are worthy of investment.*[7]

How do you approach your employees' first day of work?

Do you treat it as just another day?
Or, do you create special moments?

■ ■ ■

When Todd Whitaker wrote *What Great Principals Do Differently* in 2013, he said, *"A principal's single most precious commodity is an opening in the teaching staff."*[8] A decade later, Whitaker's words could not be truer as we navigate the worst teacher shortage in our nation's history.

Given how difficult it is to find quality teachers, one would think school leaders would do everything in their power to make a good first impression on new employees. Unfortunately, many administrators fail to capitalize on this golden opportunity. Rather than treat new teachers as their most valuable asset, leaders prioritize "more important" tasks on their calendar.

"I wish I could," say some school leaders when asked to spend more than 15 minutes with new employees, *"But I'm just too busy."*

Listen, I'm all for delegating new-teacher orientation and other onboarding tasks to subordinates. However, I continue to be amazed by how infrequently new employees report interacting with "high-level" leaders.

"You've spent more time with me today than I've ever spent with my superintendent," said one new teacher during an icebreaker activity a few years ago. *"My superintendent didn't even know my name,"* said another. Unfortunately, I've heard *dozens* of similar stories.

"I'm guessing these teachers came from large districts," you may be thinking. I thought the same thing too . . . until I asked. It ends up new teachers from small districts report *"never seeing"* their district leaders just as often as new teachers from large districts.

Again, this begs the question: *What could possibly be more important than a new employee's first day of work?*

■ ■ ■

In *The Advantage*, Patrick Lencioni shares the following:

> *The most memorable time of an employee's career, and the time with the biggest impact, are his or her first days and weeks on a new job. The impact of first impressions is just that powerful, and healthy companies take advantage of that to move new employees in the right direction.*

Leaders of organizations need to understand the value of bringing in new employees with clarity, enthusiasm, and a sense of their importance. It is an opportunity that disappears within days or weeks of a new employee's arrival and should never be wasted.[9]

The following pages contain seven ideas to consider when revamping your onboarding processes. To be clear, I'm not suggesting these ideas will eliminate your teacher-turnover issues. However, I am suggesting that the induction process deserves much more attention than most schools currently afford:

Mentoring: To help new employees feel comfortable, assign them a mentor. I'm not talking when the job begins in August . . . I'm talking the moment the employee accepts the job. Mentors in our district are expected to immediately serve as district liaisons for new employees. Having this "point person" comes in handy when new staff have questions about paperwork, schedules, and expectations in the months leading up to their start date.

Communication: In addition to assigning mentors to new teachers, leaders should also make immediate contact with new employees. As a former high school principal and current superintendent, I send each new teacher a congratulatory text shortly after they are officially hired. Furthermore, I ask them to send a personal picture to be shared on social media via our district account.

Community Introduction: Once I have the employee's picture, we create a social media post announcing the new hire. Not only does our community love seeing these pictures, new employees are often amazed by how much attention their post receives. I often tell new employees: *"I hope you're ready to become a local celebrity!"* because our community eats up these posts.

Utopia: During orientation, most schools outline a litany of expectations for new teachers. I believe we have this backward. Rather than tell them how to behave, why not ask new teachers how they wish to be treated? We do this by asking new faculty to define their "dream school"—the ideal school environment in which they want to work. With hopes of meeting these expectations, we ask new teachers how accurately their definition matches current reality during check-in meetings . . .

Check-In Meetings: Leaders must connect early and often to ensure new teachers feel supported. Whereas most administrators invest time during the first couple days . . . few administrators intentionally check in on employees once school begins. In our district, it is the expectation that both principal and superintendent complete 30-minute 1:1 meetings with each new teacher during first semester. Not only do teachers appreciate these meetings . . . I have found these conversations to be highly insightful.

Special Delivery: As was previously discussed (see page 5) our local florist delivers a school-themed plant to every new teacher on the first day of school. These gifts look great in classrooms and help new staff feel valued. To make the moment extra special, leaders should write each new teacher a personalized note explaining how lucky they are to have them in their building.

Get Real: The onboarding experience must align with the "real" culture. School leaders must ensure that the values they preach on day one match the values employees can expect year round. If your school has some work to do, *own it!* Don't be afraid to mention your weaknesses and discuss the goals you are working toward. Unfortunately, many new teachers suffer long-term shock when they realize the Pollyannaish stories they heard during orientation are much different than day-to-day reality.

■ ■ ■

During one new-teacher orientation, a teacher pulled me aside and said the following: *"Thanks for texting me after I got the job, meeting with us today, and for everything you do to make us feel important. I don't think I saw my superintendent during my three years at my previous district."*

To be fair, this teacher's previous district was much larger than ours. However, I couldn't believe this employee had never met her district leader. A few days later, I saw on social media that this particular district was dozens of teachers short to start the upcoming school year.

While it's unlikely this district's teacher shortage was a direct result of the leader's inaccessibility, it makes you wonder how many staff would stay if leadership showed genuine interest in employees.

What are you doing to make a good first impression?

Why School Leaders Must Visit Classrooms

When I meet with new leaders, they often ask how to improve their instructional leadership. Frustrated with handling discipline, returning emails, and filling out reports, these novice leaders are curious what they can do to really impact student learning.

While there are several activities they could prioritize—such as leading professional development, attending PLC meetings, or analyzing student data—one instructional leadership practice gives leaders the biggest return on investment:

Classroom walkthroughs.

■ ■ ■

As discussed in *Learning Curve,* the concept of frequent, informal observations conducted by workplace supervisors originated in 1970 when executives at Hewlett Packard implemented a concept called *Management by Wandering Around* (MBWA). The purpose of this management system—where managers became more accessible to employees by getting out of the office and into the organizational "trenches"—was to foster an environment of collaboration and trust.

Getting inside classrooms: one of the most powerful
professional practices for school leaders.

Prior to the 1970s, it was unusual for school leaders to visit class-rooms unannounced. However, after seeing the positive impact MBWA was having in other professional fields, school leaders began to implement similar strategies in their own settings.

A second turning point in walkthroughs happened in 1983 when the US Commission on Excellence in Education released *A Nation at Risk.* This landmark report asserted that American schools were "failing," touching off a wave of local, state, and federal reform efforts.

A Nation at Risk launched what is now known as the *accountability era* in schools. From *No Child Left Behind (2002),* to *Race to the Top (2009),* to the *Every Student Succeeds Act* (2015), the federal government has attempted to hold schools responsible for their quality of teaching and learning.

While accountability efforts have long been a divisive topic (many educators likely cringed while reading the last paragraph), few could argue that school reform has transformed teacher evaluation. Whereas school leaders from previous generations used a hands-off approach, today's administrators must be more proactive with teacher supervision.

Enter the classroom walkthrough.

In the early 2000s, research on classroom walkthroughs began to surface. In their 2003 Association for Supervision and Curriculum Development (ASCD) article, Margery Ginsberg and Damon Murphy identified five key benefits to walkthroughs:

Walkthroughs help administrators . . .

become familiar with teachers' instructional practices;
gauge the school culture and climate;
develop a team atmosphere;
establish themselves as instructional mentors, and
model the value of learning to students.[10]

Beyond these factors, I have discovered several associated benefits to walkthroughs during my 15 years in school leadership.

First, walkthroughs improve administrator *perception*. When administrators get out of the office and into learning spaces, they get a first-hand look at how their school operates. Not only can they observe teacher effectiveness, leaders also get a true feel for their building's culture. Furthermore, administrators who engage with staff and students in classrooms and in hallways solve many small issues before they become big headaches.

Administrators who get into classrooms improve *decision-making*. Rather than rely on second-hand information and hearsay, administrators who witness building operations with their own eyes make smarter decisions. Furthermore, school leaders who share personal observations when explaining decisions are much more likely to gain buy-in from stakeholders.

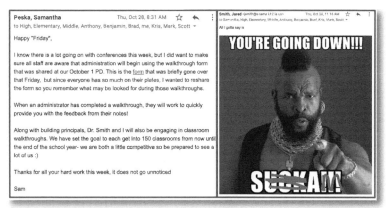

The email our curriculum director sent to teachers about walkthroughs (left). My response (right).

Walkthroughs help determine *teacher effectiveness*. Administrators who rely solely on a one-time-a-year formal observation do a huge disservice to teachers. Instead, administrators who visit classrooms several times develop a clearer picture of teacher performance. And for low-performing staff, documentation from multiple walkthroughs is ideal for plans of assistance and/or teacher removal.

Next, walkthroughs are ideal for building *teacher confidence*. Administrators should view classroom visits as a golden opportunity to highlight the specific strengths of their teachers. In a time when financial resources are limited and it's difficult to keep teachers around, few things improve retention better than well-timed, authentic, *positive* feedback from a supervisor.

Walkthroughs serve as a great *reality check*. Classroom visits can be an eye-opening and humbling experience for school leaders who have forgotten the challenges of teaching. Honest question for school administrators who continue to arbitrarily add work to teachers' plates in the postpandemic era: *How many classrooms have you visited in the last year?*

> When it comes to employee retention, few actions are more powerful than telling someone "you make a difference."
>
> #TurningPoints

Finally, walkthroughs are *therapeutic*. When I am low on energy and have a headache, visiting classrooms is the perfect remedy. Leaders who prioritize walkthroughs often find that getting into classrooms is one of the most enjoyable parts of school leadership. On numerous occasions, I have told staff that I could spend all day in their classroom. I'm not joking!

■ ■ ■

While walkthroughs are excellent for providing staff with instructional feedback, the extent to which leaders make it into classrooms is varied. While many administrators claim, *"Instructional leadership is my top priority!"* a study by the *Wallace*

Foundation revealed administrators spend less than 20% of their day engaged in this practice.[11]

What are some tips for improving walkthroughs in your setting? Here are seven ideas to consider:

Goal Setting: To avoid getting swept away by the daily whirlwind, school leaders must stay focused on their top priorities. Setting numeric walkthrough goals is one of the best ways to ensure classroom visits happen. Depending on the year, our administrators set an annual goal of 100 to 200 *documented* walkthroughs. One common mistake is forcing walkthrough numbers on administrators. Rather than saying, *"You will do 10 walkthroughs a week . . . or else!"* asking administrators to come up with target numbers increases the likelihood that goals are met.

Keeping Track: Once goals are set, administrators must develop a system for tracking their walkthroughs. One simple yet effective method is by creating a Google Sheet (spreadsheet) that includes teacher names (y-axis) and the walkthrough dates (x-axis). This format works especially well for administrative teams who want to ensure their visits are evenly distributed.

All Hands On Deck: Districts that are serious about instructional leadership create expectations for *all* licensed administrators to visit classrooms. Do you have a five-member administrative team? All five should be in classrooms. Do you work in a small district? Superintendents and curriculum directors should help pick up the slack. Walkthroughs must be a team effort, and should never be the work of one person.

Explain: Most administrators assume teachers understand how walkthroughs work. *This couldn't be further from the truth.* What data is being collected? What feedback should teachers expect? How often will visits occur? Who will visit classrooms? How will walkthroughs impact evaluations? Administrators must invest time to ensure teachers understand the walkthrough process.

Last	First	Subject/Grade	8th Visit	9th Visit
Aziz	Linda	6th Sp. Ed.	3/13/19 BA Beginning	3/21/19 BA End
Bohnstengel	Jessica	5th Grade	3/13/19 BA End	3/21/19 SB End
Coates	Carla	6th Science	3/14/19 BA Beginning	3/18/19 BA Beginning
DeBondt	Jeff	Physical Education	3/15/19 SB End	3/18/19 BA Beginning
Dixon	Derek	7th Social Studies	3/13/19 BA Beginning	3/20/19 BA Beginning
Dixon	Kristine	7th Sp. Ed.	3/15/19 BA Beginning	3/21/19 SB End
Fonua	Leah	School Counselor	3/15/19 BA End	3/18/19 BA Middle
Green	Marissa	5th Sp. Ed.	3/15/19 BA End	3/21/19 BA End
Holtz	Samantha	TAG	3/13/19 BA Middle	3/18/19 BA Beginning
Johannsen	Kelle	Sp Ed	3/15/19 BA Beginning	3/20/19 BA Beginning
Hass	Crystal	8th Grade Literacy	3/15/19 BA Beginning	3/20/19 SB Beginning
Klopping	Levi	7th Math	3/13/19 SB Beginning	3/20/19 BA Beginning
Klopping	Sarah	6th Grade Literacy	3/14/19 BA Beginning	3/18/19 BA Middle
Kokjohn	Alyson	6th Soc. Studies	3/13/19 BA Middle	3/18/19 BA Middle
Kuhter	George	8th Soc. Studies	3/14/19 BA Beginning	3/20/19 BA Beginning
McFate	Chris	Vocal Music (HS/MS)	3/15/19 SB Beginning	3/18/19 BA Middle
McFate	Morgan	M.S. STEM	3/15/19 BA Beginning	3/21/19 SB End
Miller	Paula	8th Science	3/14/19 BA Beginning	3/18/19 BA Beginning
Moore	Stacy	6-8 Sp. Ed.	3/14/19 BA Beginning	3/18/19 BA Beginning
Raue	Ashley	5th Grade	3/14/19 SB Beginning	3/20/19 BA Beginning
Smith	Kelli	5th	3/13/19 BA End	3/21/19 BA End
Smith	Teresa	5/6 Band & General Music	3/15/19 BA End	3/18/19 SB Middle
Stacey	Jeanette	8th Sp. Ed.	3/15/19 BA End	3/18/19 BA Beginning
Staff	Kory	7th Science	3/15/19 BA Beginning	3/18/19 BA Middle
Steven	Ashley	8th Math	3/14/19 BA Beginning	3/20/19 BA Beginning
Stotts	Amy	7th Int. Language Arts	3/13/19 SB Beginning	3/18/19 BA Beginning

One example of how administrators can track walkthroughs.

No Perfect Template: Notice how we have yet to talk about one specific walkthrough template. After thousands of walkthroughs, I'm convinced that *narrative feedback* is better than any complicated walkthrough form. Unless a district commits time (usually several hours) to train staff on how to interpret walkthrough feedback, complex templates leave teachers with more questions than answers. Instead, administrators should learn how to summarize their visits in a couple of short paragraphs, focusing on the actions of the teacher and the students.

Two examples of narrative feedback I've given in the past.

Stay Positive: While my narrative examples look fairly basic, in reality few administrators use this approach. Too often, administrators believe walkthroughs are a time to nitpick teacher actions. Not only does this approach destroy school culture, many faculty lose their professional confidence as a result. Given the sensitive nature of instructional feedback, districts must ensure administrators focus on positives while reserving critiques for low-performers.

Double Dip: Efficient administrators view classrooms as their second office. Rather than hide out in the office to send an email or draft a letter, why not sit in a classroom and work on those items? One of my favorite tricks as a high school principal was to complete a walkthrough and then grab a student *from that class* with whom I needed to conference. Many administrators find that their productivity skyrockets when they complete managerial work in rooms.

Instructional leadership doesn't need to be complicated. Simply getting out of the office and into the learning environment is a great first step.

And the one practice that provides leaders with the biggest return on investment?

Classroom walkthroughs.

EMPLOYEE MANAGEMENT

Look at any principal job posting and you're likely to see the following essential duty: *Manage the supervision and evaluation of teachers and other employees.*

While most will gloss over this statement, understanding how to effectively manage dozens (if not hundreds) of employees is a school leader's most important—*and most difficult*—responsibility.

Employee management is the series of activities that ensures supervisors provide employees with clarity about job expectations, as well as regular feedback about whether or not those expectations are being met.

While this process sounds straightforward, my experiences have proven otherwise.

I have made countless employee management mistakes during my 15-year administrative career. I have been accused of "harassing" some employees and "playing favorites" with others. I have been told I'm "too liberal" by some staff members and "too conservative" by others. Throw in several teacher grievances and multiple lawsuits . . . and one might wonder how I still have a job.

At first, I felt alone in my struggles: *"Do I really have what it takes to effectively manage adults?"* I wondered as another "fierce" employee conversation went sideways. However, the more I discuss this subject with other administrators, the more I realize I am not alone: employee management is a *universal issue.*

This begs the question: Why is employee management so difficult?

Much of the blame can be placed on lack of training. Despite their best efforts, college instructors struggle creating scenarios wherein students feel the emotional weight of a prickly personnel matter.

Furthermore, few districts address this important topic. Rather than coach administrators on this critical skillset, most districts waste their time with one-off trainings and "flavor-of-the-day" professional developments.

Blame can also be placed on society. Today's school culture expects supervisors to build meaningful relationships with employees while also holding them to high—if not unrealis-tic—levels of accountability. However, push too far in either direction and leaders are either a "pushover" or a "dictator" with stakeholders calling for their resignation.

Like a tightrope walker tiptoeing high above the city skyline, school leaders must walk a fine line when it comes to employee management . . . as one small misstep could end in disaster.

■ ■ ■

"Evaluation must be ongoing."

If you've worked in schools for any period of time, you've likely heard this statement. Rather than only hear feedback during the annual review, staff should be given regular performance feedback. In short, *employees should always know where they stand.*

Performance feedback can take a number of different forms. Formal classroom observations, informal classroom walkthroughs, email feedback, handwritten notes, and hallway/classroom conversations are all opportunities to provide staff with performance feedback.

Unfortunately, I have spoken with countless employees who indicate they "never" hear feedback from their administrator.

"Oh, come on . . ." I respond. *"Surely, you must get feedback from time to time?"*

"Nope," they argue. *"In fact, I can't recall the last time I had a meaningful conversation with my supervisor about my work."*

If administrators aren't spending time with employees, what exactly are they doing with their time?

As discussed in the previous chapter, the average school leader spends more than 80% of their day engaged in "managerial leadership" tasks such as student discipline, supervision, email, paperwork, and phone calls . . . leaving a small amount of time for "instructional leadership" tasks including performance feedback.

And when leaders do have time, they mistakenly assume performance feedback is unnecessary. *"My teachers know where they stand,"* some leaders will say, believing their faculty are aware of their strengths, weaknesses, and general performance levels.

"Besides," these leaders argue, *"they don't want to hear from me. They just want to be left alone."*

The data would disagree.

Whereas 96% of employees "crave" regular feedback from their employer, more than two-thirds of employees report not receiving enough feedback.[12] Furthermore, research suggests that the younger the employee, the more feedback they desire.

School leaders who get out of the office and into classrooms see employees do great things every day. However, many supervisors fail to provide teachers with timely feedback. Rather than tell the teacher: *"You crushed the lesson!"* . . . some school leaders assume the teacher already knows and simply move on with their day. Whether the feedback is verbal, handwritten, or emailed, never miss an opportunity to tell employees they are amazing. Far too many outstanding faculty question their effectiveness because they never hear positive comments from a supervisor.

Delivering constructive feedback is more challenging, as very few people enjoy telling someone: *"You can do better."* What leaders must realize is providing immediate feedback on shortcomings gives employees an opportunity to correct the problem before it's too late. And while they might initially be upset with the feedback, employees who grow from a professional critique often report a stronger relationship with their supervisor.

Providing timely, constructive criticism also eliminates the following cardinal sin: *writing negative feedback in a performance evaluation the employee has never heard before.* Not only is this unfair to the employee, this is a quick way for bosses to ruin employee relationships.

■ ■ ■

"I get what you're saying about employee management and ongoing feedback," you might be thinking. *"But I have 80 teachers and 70 support staff in my building. How do I keep it all straight?"*

Enter quarterly employee performance conversations.

Quarterly employee performance conversations are administrative team meetings where the work performance of every school employee is discussed. As a high school principal, these discussions involved myself and our four assistant principals. As a superintendent, I meet with the building principal, the building assistant principal, and director of curriculum.

To guide our meetings, we use a Google Sheet that has employees' names separated into two groups (certified staff and support staff) arranged in alphabetical order. As names are read, team members discuss strengths and weaknesses for each employee. After everyone has shared their ideas and notes are recorded, we reach a general work performance consensus for each employee.

"Wow, that sounds intense!" you may be thinking.

While this practice may sound cold-blooded, understand that these meetings are mostly positive and highly productive.

My experience is that 90 to 95 percent of school employees are competent. While their abilities range from capable to highly effective, a large majority of staff are dedicated, hard-working, and passionate about helping kids succeed.

While we could spend hours discussing our "good" employees, these conversations are normally limited due to the large number of employees we must discuss. However, we make it clear that high performers *must* continue to hear positive, work-related feedback from our team.

So, what about the "other" 5 to 10 percent of school employees—the staff who aren't working at an acceptable level? These individuals usually fall into two categories: *in need of informal coaching* or *in need of formal intervention.*

When our leadership team determines an employee has professional deficiencies, we arrange for that individual to receive informal coaching. This support is provided by an instructional coach, teacher mentor, administrator, or instructional supports outside the district.

Approximately two-thirds of the employees who receive informal coaching improve their skills to an acceptable level. However—for employees who do not improve—the next step is formal intervention, which consists of an "awareness phase" or "plan of assistance" (more on this in the next section).

The beauty of these quarterly meetings is that they force employee performance to be at the forefront of the leadership team's mind. Busy school leaders who fail to prioritize these discussions could go months without giving employees feedback.

Another benefit of these conversations is they give each administrator a voice. Far too many leadership teams defer to one person when it comes to employee evaluation, when, in reality, these need to be *team* decisions. Furthermore, collaborative discussions prevent administrators from sending mixed messages to low-performing employees.

Finally, ongoing performance discussions hold administrators accountable for addressing low-performing staff. Far too many school leaders avoid "difficult" conversations and then wonder why they experience the same personnel issues year after year. By documenting agreed-upon action steps, colleagues are held accountable for addressing the employees they have been assigned.

■ ■ ■

Speaking of low-performing staff, at some point in their career, all leaders will supervise an underperforming employee. While never fun, having the courage to address these individuals is what separates great leaders from the rest.

The following are ten basic principles for dealing with subpar employees. While I still have a lot to learn, these methods have been endorsed by educator associations, referenced by legal firms, and been featured in *School Administrator* Magazine.

Let me be clear, *by no means should the following be considered legal advice.* When dealing with employee issues in your district, consult with your human resources department or district legal counsel.

Documentation: Documenting employee concerns is a critical responsibility for school leaders. Unfortunately, many administrators lack the awareness and patience to summarize and record specific actions related to employee underperformance. In today's overly bureaucratic world, school districts must collect evidence to justify employee coaching and dismissal.

Patterns: Supervisors must focus on patterns of underperformance as opposed to single events. Aside from severe ethical and safety concerns, supervisors are required to document a series of infractions before jumping to formalized intervention. The cumulative nature of the infractions provides evidence needed to justify further remediation.

Working File: Typically an electronic file maintained by the employee's direct supervisor, the *working file* is used as a temporary holding file to archive coaching conversations and document minor employee violations. When the employee's performance or behavior warrants formal intervention or discipline, documentation should be moved from the working file to the personnel file.

Personnel File: Typically a physical file found in the district's human resources department, the *personnel file* is the employee's official work record. Significant employee concerns should be placed in this folder. Keeping documented paperwork in one location not only supports future discipline-related decisions, the file also becomes valuable during changes in leadership.

Coaching Conversations (Step 1): Leaders must offer continuous support to all employees. When supervisors notice deficiencies in performance, they (or a designee) must engage employees in *coaching conversations.* The purpose of these discussions is to develop new skills, refine existing skills, and help employees meet performance standards. Coaching documents should be placed in the employee's *working file.*

Awareness Phase and Verbal Warning (Step 2): An elevated notice of employee performance or behavior, the awareness phase and verbal warning are secondary intervention steps. The *awareness phase* addresses competency-related employee issues, while the *verbal warning* responds to behavior-related employee issues. Both documents should be placed in the employee's *working file.*

Plan of Assistance and Written Warning (Step 3): When employees are nonresponsive to coaching or their conduct is serious in nature, the plan of assistance and written warning serve as the most severe types of intervention. The *plan of assistance* is an official notice of persistent substandard performance while the *written warning* is used to document extreme behavioral misconduct. Both documents should be placed in the employee's personnel file.

Annual Evaluation: Annual evaluations reflect a complete picture of employee performance, meaning uncorrected below-standard performance must be identified in this document. As previously discussed, the annual evaluation should not be the first time the employee is made aware of deficiencies. Annual evaluations should be placed in the employee's *personnel file.*

Signature: Do employees need to sign corrective documents? While there is no "legal" requirement, best practice is to have employees sign and date remedial documents to establish a clear record of receipt. In the event an employee refuses to sign, the evaluator could write the following: *"On (Date), I handed this document to (Employee) who refused to sign acknowledging receipt. (Evaluator Signature/Date)"*

Dismissal Hearing: As the "victim mentality" continues to pervade the modern workplace, leaders must be methodical in keeping accurate documentation of employee intervention. When personnel issues reach dismissal hearings, schools must establish the employee did not respond to coaching despite being afforded several opportunities. Furthermore, schools must prove the employee is likely to continue underperformance in the future.

■ ■ ■

Before we finish, let's discuss district-level leadership. Just because this chapter has focused primarily on building administrators, please understand that these lessons also apply to superintendents and other central office leaders.

Similar to teachers, a large majority of school administrators do a terrific job. Not only do they pour their heart and soul into students and staff, most school leaders work endless hours to ensure their buildings run at high levels.

Despite their heroic efforts, it is common for school leaders to go months without receiving positive feedback from a supervisor. District leaders: How often do you deliver specific, authentic praise to principals? Did you know that the most effective leaders give five positive comments for every one negative comment?[13] If you were to track the positive and negative feedback you deliver, what would be your ratio?

Switching gears, how often have you heard the following: *"Bad principals are so hard to get rid of"*?

Put simply, *that's BS.*

Sure, administrators have bigger egos, larger paychecks, and are more likely to seek legal action. But when compared to teachers, school leaders are actually *easier* to remove thanks to limited contractual protections and multiyear probationary periods.

Unfortunately, many district leaders lack the courage to address underperforming administrators. Rather than use the steps outlined on the previous pages, they use excuses such as: *"They aren't that bad," "They are retiring soon,"* and—my favorite—*"They are untouchable."*

Listen, no underperforming employee is "untouchable." Quit trying to justify your lack of action and *do the work*.

Superintendents: Don't criticize principals for keeping ineffective teachers when you don't have the guts to remove ineffective administrators. And please don't complain about how "difficult" or "stressful" your job is when you don't have the backbone to remove poor leaders.

Your job is "difficult" or "stressful" because you're always cleaning up the messes left by the poor leaders you continue to employ.

> **Superintendents:**
>
> Please don't complain about how "difficult" or "stressful" your job is when you don't have the backbone to remove poor leaders.
>
> Your job is "difficult" or "stressful" because you're always cleaning up the messes left by the poor leaders you continue to employ.
>
> #TurningPoints

■ ■ ■

Kathryn Minshew, CEO and cofounder of *The Muse*, said the following: "*Done right, a performance review is one of the best opportunities to encourage and support high performers and constructively improve your middle- and lower-tier workers.*"

This is the essence of effective employee management.

School leaders who embrace the principles outlined in this chapter not only lay the foundation for a positive culture, they also establish an atmosphere of high expectations.

SYSTEMS OF COMMUNICATION

Amazing things happen in schools every day.

Each building is full of support staff, teachers, and administrators who devote every ounce of their energy to doing what is best for kids.

As schools continue to do more with less, educators rise to the challenge to ensure students receive the education, guidance, and support needed for success.

Unfortunately, most of what happens inside schools goes no further than classroom walls. In a world with countless distractions, schools struggle to build community awareness of the happenings within their buildings.

Whereas some schools do a great job of sharing their story, many have struggled to adjust to the ever-changing communication landscape. But rather than take ownership of their poor messaging, many school leaders are quick to blame everyone *but* themselves:

"We sent a letter home!"
"Why don't they look at the website?"
"They don't read their email."

"It's posted on Facebook . . ."
"Students don't listen."
"Parents don't care."

School leaders must understand that a school's image, reputation, and credibility depend on clear, consistent communication. Whereas previous generations naturally trusted the educational system, today's schools are no longer given the benefit of the doubt. When schools neglect communication, the community fills in the gaps with their own (often negative) opinions and conclusions with the little information they have.

In the 1980s, political consultant Lee Atwater began using the phrase: *"Perception is reality."* Who could have guessed that 40 years later those words would define American schools?

■ ■ ■

Let's take a moment to discuss communication during these "unprecedented times." Certainly, these last few years have been anything but normal for school leaders. Mask mandates, book bans, bathroom access, litter boxes . . . schools have been caught in the crossfire of many cultural issues.

Scroll through social media or flip through the local newspaper and it's hard not to notice headlines such as: *"School Board Meeting Erupts Over Mask Mandate"* and *"Teachers Threaten Resignation Over Banned Books."* As often as these stories appear, one would assume chaos and confusion are unavoidable.

However, further investigation reveals that upset parents and angry teachers are rarely the root cause of school issues. Instead, many districts are guilty of creating their own crises because they ignore best practices in organizational communication.

Consider the districts in your region that have experienced staff and community backlash. Have those leaders followed these fundamental practices?

Collaboration: Do leaders ask staff what is feasible in their setting?

Buy-In: Do leaders generate support prior to making decisions?

Transparency: Do leaders explain the decision-making process?

No Surprises: Do leaders give staff and parents time to prepare for changes?

Humility: Do leaders put their egos aside when making decisions?

Certainly, some issues are unavoidable. Some districts have dysfunctional school boards with political agendas, while others have crazy parent groups who oppose every district decision.

However, school leaders do themselves no favors when they ignore the basic rules of effective communication.

■ ■ ■

School leaders at every level must prioritize clear, timely, and transparent communication. From district superintendents to building principals to teacher leaders, sustained systemic success requires effective messaging.

Leaders who openly share information empower staff. When information funnels up and down an organization in a free-flowing manner, all employees feel like a part of the team. In times when employees are difficult to find, communication is crucial for recruitment, engagement, and retainment.

External communication also plays a significant role in school success, meaning leaders must implement systems for sharing information with parents and the community.

"Who cares what the community thinks?" some leaders may argue. *"I could care less about public perception!"*

Unfortunately, this old-school mentality limits a school leader's influence.

A direct correlation exists between school communication and public trust. The better a school communicates with the public, the more the public trusts the school. And the more the public trusts the school, the more likely the public is willing to forgive when issues emerge.

Think of this relationship like a bank account. With each message, schools make tiny deposits of trust that accumulate over time. Building up this bank account is crucial when adversity strikes a district. Schools that stockpile social capital build immunity to public attacks, whereas schools with depleted reserves become vulnerable to community backlash.

Whereas communication can make or break a school, few districts develop systems for effective stakeholder communication. Why does this happen? Here are five common school leader excuses:

"Our communication is just fine." When questioned about their messaging, many school leaders stubbornly insist no changes are needed. Unfortunately, recent studies signal a significant disconnect between leaders' perceptions of communication and the levels of communication stakeholders experience.[14]

Whereas isolated mentions of positive school experiences may seem trivial, over time these references begin to add up.

As more individuals feel compelled to share their story, positive messaging begins to permeate the public's awareness.

Eventually, the entire community becomes energized by the school's positive energy.

#TurningPoints

"Communication doesn't impact student achievement." Wrong. Clear communication leads to parent engagement, and parent engagement impacts student outcomes. Children whose parents are actively engaged in the school environment are more likely to have higher grades and test scores, better attendance, better social skills, and better behavior . . . regardless of family income or background.[15]

"Volunteers run our external communications." Schools are notorious for asking employees to volunteer their time to manage the school website and social media pages. As an assistant principal I pleaded with the "higher ups" to pay these individuals, but each time I was told no. *No wonder our communication sucked.*

The average school district runs a $50 million dollar budget . . . why not spend a few dollars on communication?

"We have kids run our external communications." Along the same lines of *"let's find volunteers"* is the *"let's have kids do it"* line. Don't get me wrong, I love empowering students and giving them ownership of projects. However, school leaders who are serious about creating *effective systems of communication* understand this responsibility cannot be delegated to the school's digital media class.

"We don't have money for a communications director." Most large school districts have the capacity to hire a communications director or communications team to handle messaging. But what about smaller districts? As a high school principal and a super-intendent, I formed a communications team to ensure our story was told. My previous district had eleven (!!) communications team members. Some staff are given stipends, while others have communicative roles woven into their job responsibilities. Total cost to the district? Roughly $10,000 per year.

■ ■ ■

In *Culturize*, Jimmy Casas says the following:

> *Many of the issues schools face today are deeply embedded in how people communicate, neglect to communicate in a timely fashion, or fail to communicate all together. Most of the negativity, harsh feelings, and unnecessary work that is endured in schools can be tied back to poor communication.*[16]

Consider the current issues within your school or district. Are these problems the result of an *"unexpected crisis"*? Or, are these problems the result of poor communication?

MEET OUR

STC
COMMUNICATION
TEAM

JARED SMITH
Superintendent
- Oversee communications
- Communicate information to staff and the community
- Gather feedback for improving communication
- Make decisions about weather and other cancellations

STEVE BEARDEN
Director of Social Media
- Oversee district Facebook, Twitter, and Instagram
- Post staff and community photos/stories on social media
- Encourage staff and community to send information and follow our pages.
- Updates all social media pages

STEPHANIE LANE
Director of Graphic Design
- Create graphics and digital images for staff
- Photo editing & photo graphics
- Create infographics
- T-Shirt Design
- Other miscellaneous designs

MARY MIXDORF
Director of Technology
- Oversee STC website
- Maintain/update District & Partnership Center webpages
- Update communication forms & documents
- Oversees JMC
- Updates all social media pages

ANTHONY JAHR, SCOTT BOLEN, CHELSEA AHRENS
Activities
- Updates calendar of events
- Communicate activities updates & cancellations
- Oversee event livestream
- Share activities updates, scores, pictures
- Update the high school digital sign

LAURA GALVEZ
District Translator
- Translate all messages (including social media and website) to Spanish
- Translate documents that go to families
- Send Spanish voice messages in JMC

HEATHER GARRETT, CRYSTAL HASS, VICTORIA HAMILTON
Building Level Webmasters
- Oversee building web pages
- Post pictures and documents on the website
- Handle building level announcements

In a time when schools face intense scrutiny, school leaders must stop with the excuses and develop systems to effectively share their story.

OMG—It's Happening!

Today's school leaders are dealing with more bureaucracy and political pressure than ever before.

For example, during the COVID outbreak, school leaders were asked to interpret rulings and make decisions while politicians argued over how to handle the pandemic. Whether it was virtual learning, student masking, contact tracing, or staff vaccinations . . . something "urgent" was always being asked of schools.

Clearly, these were (and continue to be) important topics. Leaders must be careful to understand the social and political landscape to ensure they avoid legal trouble. However, some school leaders get so consumed with the actions of local and federal legislators that they lose focus of what really matters: *the employees they serve.*

■ ■ ■

On November 5, 2021, OSHA published an Emergency Temporary Standard (ETS) mandating that companies with 100 or more staff *"require all employees get fully vaccinated against COVID or be required to wear a face covering and undergo weekly testing."* [17]

When this "mandate" was announced, many school leaders dropped everything and immediately began enforcing new policies and procedures. Just like Michael Scott yelling, *"Oh my God—it's happening!"* in the classic "Fire Drill" scene from *The Office*, many school leaders sprang from their desks and quickly alarmed staff of forthcoming changes.

While leaders thought an immediate response was necessary, this knee-jerk reaction backfired in many districts. Rather than put staff at ease, their actions did nothing but raise questions and create tension.

On November 12, 2021, the US Court of Appeals ordered that OSHA, *"Take no steps to implement or enforce"* the ETS *"until further court order."* A short time later, OSHA *"suspended activities related to the implementation and enforcement of the ETS pending future developments in the litigation."*

Only a few days removed from telling staff: *"Get vaccinated . . . or else!"* administrators had to reverse course and inform employees that the mandate was overturned. While some leaders apologized to staff, most brushed it off as "politics" and moved on with their week, as if to say, *"No harm, no foul."*

I beg to differ.

This leadership behavior is incredibly harmful to staff and is a primary reason why stress levels in schools are at all-time highs.

Far too many leaders believe they have to immediately react to everything that the "state" and "feds" say. Rather than take a wait-and-see approach, many leaders emphatically tell staff a mandate must be followed. *"Making sure we stay out of legal trouble is our top priority,"* these leaders proclaim.

But *should* it be their top priority?

If school leaders asked employees: *"What should be our top priority?"*, themes such as staff burnout and teacher shortage would likely top the list. In fact, I doubt "following legislative mandates" would even register.

Ironically, school leaders who stress enforcement of political directives do nothing but compound staff burnout and teacher shortage issues.

■ ■ ■

In *The Effective Executive*, Peter Drucker suggests that leaders must:

> *Identify time-wasters by looking for the recurrent "crisis." This is a crisis that comes back year after year. A crisis that recurs a second time is a crisis that must not occur again. A recurrent crisis should have always been foreseen. The recurrent crisis is simply a symptom of sloppiness and laziness.*[18]

Rather than treat every political "mandate" as a crisis, school leaders should remain calm and follow a series of steps when new legislation is announced. The following are seven ideas to consider:

Gather Input: When new mandates are announced, school leaders should discuss those decisions with their leadership team. But rather than *tell* what will be done, school leaders must ask their lieutenants for feedback by asking questions such as: *"How might this mandate impact your building and the employees you supervise?"*, *"Do you believe this mandate is feasible?"*, and *"What blind spots do I have when looking at this mandate?"*

Informal Conversations: School leaders cannot make informed decisions from the comforts of their office. Informed decisions only happen when school leaders visit the trenches of their organization. Prior to enforcing state mandates, empathetic leaders listen to employee perspectives by asking, *"What are your thoughts about this mandate?"* and *"How could this mandate affect your job?"*

Connect with Other Districts: When new mandates are announced, administrators should reach out to their professional network to understand how rulings are playing out in other districts. Asking, *"Are we making a decision that is consistent with other schools or are we an outlier?"* serves as valuable data when leaders are asked to make difficult decisions.

District	Plan for Mandatory Vaccine Policy	When Will Decision be Made?	Other Notes about Plans
Solon	Wait & See	will only place in handbook if needed	Anticipating a win in the courts to prevent the overreach so not worried about the need to implement
Independence	Wait & See	will only place in handbook if needed, will hold a special Board meeting in December if need be.	Same as Solon but working behind the scenes to prepare for possible implementation
W. Delaware	Wait & See	IASB policy is ready, but will hold a special meeting to adopt it only if needed because the stay is lifted.	
CPU	Wait & See	Will place on board agenda if the stay is changed.	Same as Solon & Indy.
CCA			
Marion	Other	Adding policy language to our staff handbook rather than board policy. Board to approve handbook update during Nov 22 mtg, but will only implement if it is required	Created form in our HR system for staff to voluntarily disclose vaccination status and upload copy of card. If this becomes a mandate we will use same system (Frontline) to track weekly tests, which will be staff member responsibility
Benton	Wait and See	Have sent IASB's policies out to Board before our Nov. 22 mtg. As of Nov. 22, Board tabled the policies for now. Will wait and see	Concern is OSHA is req'r to have policy in place by Dec. 6. and whether or not this is enforceable. (Employers must comply with most provisions on prior slide by December 6, 2021 except for testing requirement, which will be required on Jan 4, 2022) https://drive.google.com/file/d/1AOBu1fiepk8mfipkrOpVW1sEaL8LzT8/view?usp=sharing
Williamsburg		If the stay is lifted, we'll take the exemplar policies to the board.	Starting to get the mechanisms in place to collect the information. Very preliminary work.
Beckman	Wait & See	TBD—Waiting for guidance from archdiocese	We are under 100 employees as an individual school but if schools are included together in the archdiocese as one unit we will be over 100 employees.
Vinton-Shells	Wait & See	Would not place on board agenda until the stay is changed.	Would adopt OHSA sample policy if needed. Would use our Talent Ed HR program for tracking.
Mount Vernon			
South Tama			
Maquoketa			

This Google Sheet was sent to all superintendents in our conference for feedback.

Summarize Data: Once conversations with leaders, employees, and other districts have occurred, administrators should interpret the data. If the feedback to a particular mandate is generally supportive, leaders should be good to move forward. But if the feedback to a particular mandate is strongly opposed, the school leader must consider alternative options.

Remove Feelings: Rather than make decisions based on personal opinions, administrators must make decisions that reflect the opinions of their stakeholders. While their actions may be commendable, countless school leaders have lost their jobs as a result of making decisions based on their political allegiances as opposed to genuinely listening to the views of the school community.

School Board: In many cases, mandates must go before the board. When this happens, district leaders should err on the side of advocating for employees. Even if the board goes against your wishes (which has happened to me many times), word of your actions will spread and a groundswell of support from employees will follow.

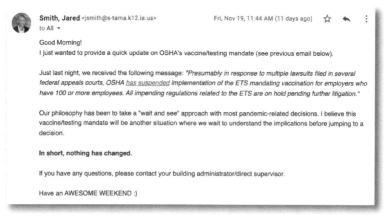

Smith, Jared <jsmith@s-tama.k12.ia.us>   Fri, Nov 19, 11:44 AM (11 days ago)
to All

Good Morning!
I just wanted to provide a quick update on OSHA's vaccine/testing mandate (see previous email below).

Just last night, we received the following message: *"Presumably in response to multiple lawsuits filed in several federal appeals courts, OSHA has suspended implementation of the ETS mandating vaccination for employers who have 100 or more employees. All impending regulations related to the ETS are on hold pending further litigation."*

Our philosophy has been to take a "wait and see" approach with most pandemic-related decisions. I believe this vaccine/testing mandate will be another situation where we wait to understand the implications before jumping to a decision.

In short, nothing has changed.

If you have any questions, please contact your building administrator/direct supervisor.

Have an AWESOME WEEKEND :)

Reassure Staff: Once a decision is made, leaders must provide updates to employees. Far too often, administrators shy away from sending all-staff communications for fear of spamming inboxes. Instead, leaders must remember *there is no such thing as overcommunication.* Furthermore, administrators should view these messages as opportunities to explain how their leadership philosophy plays a role in decision-making.

■ ■ ■

I have sometimes been criticized for being too laid back when it comes to "mandates."

However, I'm willing to shoulder this criticism if it means employees are shielded from bureaucratic drama.

School leaders: Please stop treating every political "mandate" as a crisis. Rather than worry about lawmakers in a faraway city, focus on the employees you serve.

School Leaders: Please stop treating every political "mandate" as a crisis.

Rather than worry about lawmakers in a far-away city, focus on the employees you serve.

#TurningPoints

"I'M CALLING MY LAWYER!"

"I'm Calling My Lawyer!"

Educational leaders hear this all the time. Often, these statements come from upset parents who believe schools mishandled a situation with their child. Sometimes, the threats are from employees who believe they were wronged by the district. Occasionally, they come from students who believe they were mistreated by staff.

In most cases, *"I'm calling my lawyer!"* declarations go nowhere.

But what happens when a parent, employee, or student actually follows through? What can you expect?

The first time I discovered someone was taking legal action as a direct result of my handling of a situation, I was paranoid. I was in my fifth year as a school administrator—and although many angry individuals had threatened to contact a lawyer—this was the first time someone carried out their promise.

When I found out the individual had taken legal action, many thoughts went through my head:

"Who exactly is getting sued?"
"Will I have to pay money?"
"What can I do to fight this?"

158

"Am I going to get fired?"
"Will I go to court?"

While I am a natural worrier, I was worried for good reason: *No one ever told me what happens when people take legal action against you.* Not once was this topic discussed in my educational leadership coursework, administrative mentoring program, or as an administrative team.

Sure, we had discussed the "classic" school law cases (Brown v. Board of Education, Tinker v. Des Moines, etc.) in our master's classes, but never did we talk about what happens when you—*the school leader*—find yourself in a legal battle.

The following paragraphs share key ideas about the litigation process. My hope is these concepts fill in the blanks for what others have failed to mention, while helping you avoid the distress I've experienced in my personal journey.

■ ■ ■

Educational leaders must understand that schools are no longer given the benefit of the doubt. Whereas in the past they may have taken responsibility for their actions . . . parents, employees, and students have discovered it's much easier to blame the school. So, when things aren't going their way in a disagreement with school officials, these people resort to: *"I'm calling my lawyer!"* as the ultimate mic drop.

And who could blame them? Leaders who enter the profession are quickly introduced to a world of bureaucracy. Rather than be trusted to use their professional judgment, school leaders are told they must follow employee handbooks, school board policies, and state code. Throw in the volatile health, political, and social justice landscape, and it's nearly impossible for school leaders to know what they *should be doing.*"

Certainly, there are times when legal action is necessary. I cringe when I see the unethical and inequitable treatment of parents, employees, and students in some school districts. When I come across these horrific stories, I can't help but cheer for those who have the courage to stand up against these examples of inept leadership.

But what about the rest of us? What about those who are genuinely trying to do what is best for students and employees?

Unfortunately, even the most meticulous rule-followers are sitting ducks for lawyers and their clients. In addition to the laundry list of procedures that must be flawlessly executed, school districts are juicy targets for lawyers because of one thing: *money.*

"Money?" you may be thinking. *"There's no money in schools!"*

Whereas most educators believe schools are underfunded, this does not diminish the fact that schools are *multimillion-dollar organizations.* In the United States, total expenditures for public elementary and secondary schools are approximately $800 billion.[19] When divided across roughly 14,000 school districts nationwide, the average public school district operates a budget north of $50 million.

To summarize: *unrealistic standards + guaranteed funding = easy target for litigation*

The numbers support this claim. Between 1907 and 1976, federal cases litigated against schools increased by 550%.[20] More recently, federal civil rights lawsuits against districts doubled between 2013 and 2017.[21] Incidentally, websites such as *How Do I Sue a School District?* and *How to Sue a School: 8 Reasons You Should* provide step-by-step advice for individuals looking to sue a district.

What a time to be alive.

■ ■ ■

So, let's say you suddenly find yourself entangled in a legal situation. What can you expect? Below are five general takeaways from my personal experiences. Keep in mind that every state and situation is different:

"Who exactly is getting sued?" If you were the school leader responsible for the event in question, a good chance exists you will be named—along with the school district—in the lawsuit. While this is scary, understand that most school leaders experience at least one lawsuit naming them as a defendant during their career. Even more important, realize that school leaders are not individually responsible for any settlement or monetary award in most cases.

"Will I have to pay money?" Assuming you haven't made a colossal error in judgment, take comfort in knowing that districts cover lawsuit costs. Schools have special funds—separate from the all-important *general fund*—designed to pay for legal settlements. Attorney fees and other costs associated with lawsuits are also covered using these funds or the district's liability insurance carrier.

"What can I do to fight this?" When dealing with a lawsuit, school leaders will be asked to provide documentation of

the incident. Therefore, it's vital that they get in the habit of proactively keeping detailed notes of situations that could potentially lead to litigation. *"Well, I'm just going to go back and write down what happened,"* you might think upon being named in a lawsuit. Unfortunately, legal counsel will be asking for *contemporaneous notes,* that is documentation made at the time or shortly after an event occurs. Detailing what happened several months after the incident will likely carry less weight in the eyes of the judge.

"Am I going to get fired?" Rarely do school leaders lose their job as a result of a single litigation. Obviously, we can all think of extreme cases when school employees make enormous mistakes, resulting in loss of licensure or a vote of no confidence from the school board. But those incidents are few and far between. Rather than fear for their job, school leaders should use lawsuits as learning opportunities and commit to avoiding similar mistakes in the future.

"Will I go to court?" Only 5% of civil lawsuits actually make it to court, meaning most school leaders will never participate in a trial. What happens the other 95% of the time? Best case scenario: The judge throws out the lawsuit. In many situations, the school district will reach a monetary settlement with the plaintiff.

"Wait—most school districts reach settlements?" you may be thinking. *"What if you did nothing wrong?"*

This is quite possibly the most important takeaway of this chapter. Even when school leaders follow best practice and keep detailed documentation, it is still likely a settlement will be reached with the plaintiff. In these cases, settlements are reached for *nuisance value*, which is to avoid allocating time and financial resources away from student learning to defend a lawsuit.

School leaders often take things personally when a settlement is reached. This is understandable because of the perception that a settlement is an admission of guilt. However, you must realize that our culture—and legal system—support the victim mentality more than ever.

In short, lawsuits are the cost of doing business in schools today.

■ ■ ■

Several months after I was named as a defendant in a lawsuit for the first time, I heard the school district settled with the individual. At the time, I felt terrible about my mistake.

However, now I use this case as a valuable turning point in my career development.

Not only did I learn how to avoid getting into the same situation in the future . . . I also learned that lawsuits are an unfortunate—and oftentimes *unavoidable*—way of life for school leaders.

Learn from Your Failures

One of a school leader's most important responsibilities is guiding the community through a process of asking for money for building projects. Given they generate very little income on their own, most school districts are reliant on their communities to help cover the cost of construction projects.

A *bond referendum* is a voting process that allows community members to decide if a school district is authorized to raise property taxes for the purpose of building new schools and improving existing facilities. Similar to a house mortgage, a *bond* gives school districts the ability to finance new projects without actually having the money at the time of purchase. When a bond referendum passes, the school district uses the increase in property tax to pay back the bond over several years.

In affluent communities, bond referendums are fairly straightforward. Most community members don't mind paying a little extra for community development, and will vote "yes" on a school project without thinking twice.

Conversely, in working-class communities, bond referendums are more difficult to pass. Given that citizens in blue-collar towns have less disposable income, they are more likely to push back on projects that require taxpayer money.

I had the opportunity to lead a working-class community through two bond referendums with drastically different outcomes. This chapter shares what I learned through my experiences, pinpointing differences between the votes while providing tips for school leaders who undertake similar projects.

■ ■ ■

The South Tama County (STC) School District is located in central Iowa, about an hour northeast of Des Moines. The district spans 262 square miles, with a majority of its 10,000 residents living in the towns of Tama and Toledo.

Although it might sound like a typical Iowa district, STC is noted for its cultural diversity. A large Hispanic and Native American population makes STC one of the few "majority-minority" school districts in Iowa.

Approximately 65% of the students who attend South Tama County qualify for free or reduced lunches. With a median household income of roughly $49,000, the average STC family makes 20% less than the average Iowa family ($61,500 median) and 25% less than the average American family ($67,000 median).[22]

The three largest employers in the community are the Meskwaki Casino Hotel, the Iowa Premium meat packing plant, and the STC School District. Agriculture plays a predominant role in the area, as local employers cater to farmers who harvest the surrounding land. Small businesses also make up a large portion of the workforce, although some have closed their doors in the postpandemic era.

Similar to other small towns, STC has an aging population. The average resident in the community is 43 years old, compared to Des Moines (34), Iowa City (26) and Ames (23)—all of which are a short drive away. With more job choices and social opportunities, many young adults choose to leave the community.

This combination of limited resources, sluggish economy, and aging population result in a fiscally conservative community that mirrors many small towns across the country. As a result, when citizens are asked to approve property tax increases to fund school projects, these requests are often met with resistance.

Recent voting history speaks to this general resistance.

In 2013, the school district asked the community to raise the local tax levy to assist with repairs and maintenance on school buildings. Needing a 50% majority to pass, the 2013 vote fell a single vote short of passing.

In 2014, the school district asked the community to raise the local tax levy once again. However, this proposal was met with even greater resistance, garnering only 41% of the vote.

By the time I was named superintendent in 2018, focus had shifted to the aging middle school. Built in the early 1900s, the school was over 100 years old and nearing the end of its usable life. In addition to being one of the oldest operating buildings in the state, the middle school needed significant updating to meet state code requirements.

In 2020, we asked district taxpayers to vote on a bond referendum to pay for a new middle school.

"Slow down!" you might be thinking. *"First you said 'levy.' Now you're saying 'bond.' What is the difference?"*

Great question. While levies and bonds both use taxpayer money to raise revenue, they use different approaches to get there.

Think of *levies* like checking accounts, meaning money is spent *after* taxpayer money has been collected. Since they are not taking on debt, districts pay no interest and make no repayments. In contrast, recall that *bonds* are like mortgages, meaning money is spent *before* taxpayer money has been collected. Since they are taking on debt, districts pay interest and make annual or semiannual payments.

Another difference between levies and bonds is the voter-approval process. In many states, levies are easier to approve than bonds. For example, Iowa requires a 50% simple majority for levies to be approved, while bonds require a 60% supermajority. And while 10% doesn't sound like much, this gap can be difficult for districts to overcome . . . which brings us back to 2020.

When we asked our community to approve a bond for a new middle school in 2020, 54% of the community voted "yes." While a majority of the community supported the project, we didn't get the 60% supermajority needed to approve the bond.

At first, I was bummed about the result. Losing isn't fun—especially when it comes to something that required so much time and energy. *"Maybe they were right,"* I thought upon recalling the numerous community members who had warned that a school project will *"never pass."*

Then I was reminded of the following quote by Henry Ford: *"The only real mistake is the one from which we learn nothing."*

Rather than blame the community and complain about circumstances outside our control, we focused on what could be learned from the previous vote. Armed with a tremendous team of architects, engineers, tax experts, and communication specialists, we spent the next two years preparing for another opportunity.

When we reengaged the community in conversations about the middle school, building trust was our top priority. This meant approaching each conversation with a tone of *vulnerability*. By owning up to our mistakes during the 2020 vote—and explaining how this vote would be different—we aimed to restore confidence in the school district.

Our efforts paid off.

Community members grew increasingly supportive of the revamped project. They liked that we had listened to their concerns and made changes based on their feedback. As the vote neared, there was growing confidence that a building project could pass for the first time in nearly two decades.

When word spread that the vote had passed, we weren't surprised. What did surprise us was the level at which the vote had passed: *a whopping 83%*.

Not only had we doubled community support in eight short years, the 83% approval rate was the *highest percentage* of any bond voted upon in Iowa during the spring of 2022.

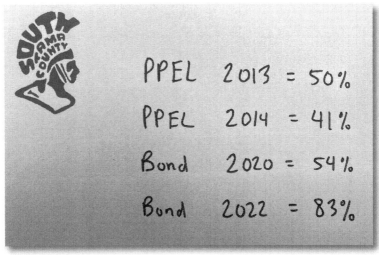

PPEL 2013 = 50%

PPEL 2014 = 41%

Bond 2020 = 54%

Bond 2022 = 83%

The high-tech graphic I shared on social media after the bond passed.

■ ■ ■

Whereas the previous paragraphs make the process sound simple, few things consume more of a district leader's time than a building project. And while I will spare you the finer details, the most important thing I learned while leading a district through two bond votes was that the *rules for generating support are universal*, meaning that the best practices used to generate employee support on work issues are the same best practices used to generate community support on bond issues.

During the first vote, I abandoned these best practices. Thinking that garnering public support required a different skillset, I took bad advice and tried approaches that I would never do with employees. And when the results weren't what we had hoped, I shouldn't have been surprised.

During the second vote, I revisited these best practices. Rather than behave differently because we were engaging the community,

I fell back on the methods used to generate support with employees. And while bond votes depend on several factors, this revised approach was vital to our success.

What are those "best practices?" Here are six ideas to consider:

Empower Those Affected by the Decision: When decisions are made, the voices of those affected by the decision must be heard. One mistake we made during the 2020 vote was that most decisions were made by school leadership as opposed to community members. Learning from this mistake, we created a task force and empowered community members to make project decisions (location, cost, etc.) while removing school leadership from those conversations.

All Voices at the Table: During the 2020 vote, I was reluctant to involve anyone critical of the school district in the decision-making process. *"Positive supporters only!"* I demanded. However, during the 2022 vote we invited citizens who were notoriously opposed to property tax increases to be on the task force. To my surprise, these individuals turned out to be some of our most loyal supporters.

Don't Take Things Personally: When empowering others to make decisions, leaders can't take things personally. Leading up to the 2022 vote, some committee members made comments that felt like an attack on my leadership. *"The district doesn't communicate well with the older generation"* and *"The district doesn't explain how property taxes work"* were two complaints. As much as these opinions hurt, I bit my tongue and made changes based on their feedback.

It Goes Down in the DM: Strong communication is vital for running a successful bond project. During both the 2020 and

2022 votes, we used a wide variety of communication tools, including social media, snail mail, and the local newspaper. However, marketing research indicates that text messages are read 98% of the time, compared to only 20% for email.[23] With this in mind, we placed added emphasis on text messaging during the 2022 vote.

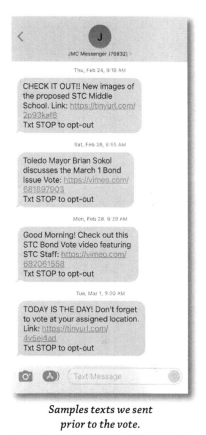

Samples texts we sent prior to the vote.

Answer All Questions: In 2020, I did a poor job answering the community's questions about the project. This led to stakeholders feeling like information was intentionally being withheld. In 2022, we committed to answering all community questions in a timely manner. By creating a website with a lengthy FAQ page—as well as funneling questions to our team of "experts" (architects, engineers, finance, tax, etc.)—we built considerable trust by following through on every community request.

Look at this Photograph: During the 2020 vote, I was advised not to share too many renderings of the middle school project as the community could nitpick minor details. *This was a mistake.* During the 2022 vote, we switched gears and asked architects to produce several photos. Not only did the public love these visuals, each new photo release created a positive buzz in the community that lasted for days.

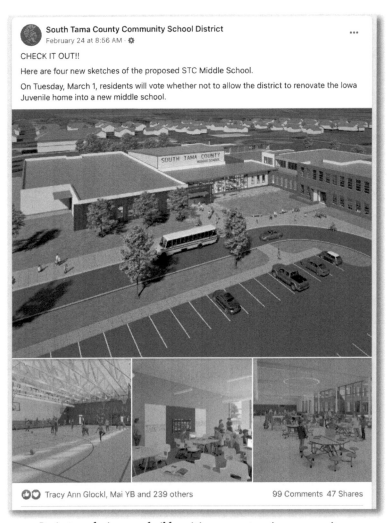

Project renderings can build positive momentum in a community.

■ ■ ■

When I arrived at South Tama County, community members feared that a bond referendum would never pass. Due to mistrust of school leadership, tough economic times, and division in the community, most people believed a new middle school was nothing but a pipe dream.

After the 2020 vote, I began to have similar thoughts. *"What if we never pass a bond vote?"* I worried.

However—once I realized that the *rules for generating support are universal*—I felt much better about our chances.

Don't make my same mistake: rather than assume generating community support requires a different approach, fall back on the same principles you would use to generate buy-in with employees.

SCHOOL'S OUT FOR THE SUMMER!

Ahhhhh . . . the last day of work.

Kids are gone, grades are submitted, rooms are packed, and summer break is imminent.

On this final day, school leaders have a decision:

Do I keep teachers to the end of the day?
Or, do I let teachers go early?

At first blush, a few hours of work seems trivial. But in reality, this decision speaks volumes about the way teachers are treated.

■ ■ ■

As a high school principal, one annual tradition was a golf outing on the last day of work. This event was less about playing golf (I am a *terrible* golfer) and more about spending time with colleagues in a social setting.

Hoping to play nine holes before it got too late, our social committee set up tee times for 4:00pm. When the plan was shared with me, committee members were curious if I would allow staff to leave earlier than their "contracted" time of 3:30pm.

To me, the answer was obvious: of course they could leave early.

"In fact, why don't we let staff go after lunch?" I offered.

"Well, we might get into trouble," said one committee member. *"And what will the district office think? Plus, the community might wonder why we aren't at work . . ."*

"You guys worked hard all year long," I responded. *"I know staff has put in far more hours than their 'contracted time.' The least we can do is let them leave a few hours early."*

Not only did we allow staff to leave after lunch, I publicized the event and encouraged employees to attend the golf outing. Even if they didn't play, I encouraged them to ride in a cart or hang out in the clubhouse. I also convinced our administrative team to cover a $300 tab at the "19th Hole."

As a superintendent, I used a similar approach to the last day of work. Prior to assuming the role, it was expected that staff stay the full contracted day. So—when I inquired about staff leaving early—similar questions arose: *"We've never done that before,"* said one employee. *"Is that fair for all staff members?"* said another.

Again, I pushed back on these concerns: *"I hear what you are saying,"* I responded. *"But I feel like staff would really appreciate this gesture. If it helps, think of an early dismissal as 'trade time' that has accumulated over the year."*

Not only did we allow staff to leave early, we worked with local businesses to organize an all-staff tailgate to end the year in style. Complete with limitless burgers, brats, and fixings, summertime music (cue "Kokomo" by The Beach Boys) and a "bags" tournament, this was one last opportunity for staff to congregate before leaving for summer break. Furthermore, I shared plans of an informal gathering at a local "restaurant" following lunch and encouraged employees to attend.

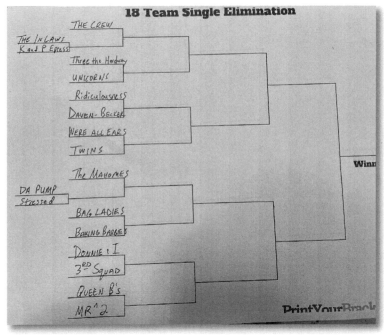

The bags tournament bracket—our staff was pretty competitive!

"What's the big deal?" noneducators may be thinking. *"We let employees go early all the time."*

Whereas it is common for private sector employees to work shortened hours (when was the last time *you* saw the dentist on a Friday afternoon?), the prevailing opinion is that educators must fulfill every minute of their contract.

Obviously, most school jobs require that staff be in the presence of children, meaning employees can't just come and go as they please. However, school leaders who understand the importance of time and approach the concept with an open mind typically have no problem finding occasional opportunities to let staff leave early.

Scenes from the 2021 and 2022 STC Bags Tournament

■ ■ ■

Thinking about letting staff leave early in your own setting? Here are five common barriers, with a response to each:

"But you're not following the contract!" Some people will argue when school employees are allowed to leave early that the district is "wasting taxpayer money." I would argue that school employees routinely work far more hours than is indicated on their contract. Leaders should consider these early dismissals as "trade time" that staff accumulate over the course of a year.

"But the community will complain!" Some may worry that if school employees are seen at the golf course or local "establishment" before 4:00pm, community members will grumble. I have supported these activities for 15 years and have yet to field one complaint. *"Happy Hour"* is part of the modern work culture and is readily accepted in most professions (both of my business-world brothers often enjoy happy hour drinks *in* the office!). If people still want to complain . . . invite them to spend a day in a classroom.

"But they have work to do!" If you think the last contracted day is when "important" work needs to be done, think again. Unfortunately, many districts believe they need to squeeze every ounce of work out of employees before summer break. While extensive end-of-the-year professional learning and data reflection sounds reasonable, forcing work down the throats of already-checked-out teachers on their last day is a terrible idea.

"But what about the other schools?" Depending on district office philosophy, school leaders could find themselves in hot water allowing staff to leave early while other schools keep staff until the end of the day. Keep in mind that the larger the district, the more likely your school can fly under the radar. When I worked in one of the 600-plus Chicago Public schools, we could have told staff to stay home on the last day of work and no one would have noticed. While every district is different, building leaders who have the courage to make sensible, staff-friendly decisions earn loyalty from employees.

"But what about hourly staff?" When teachers are told they can leave early on the last day (or other days), it's easy to forget the custodians, secretaries, and other hourly staff. What is difficult

is that hourly employee pay is governed by the punch clock or time cards. While all situations are different, classified employees should be encouraged to leave with the teachers and get paid for the hours they miss. Not only will this ensure that hourly employees feel valued, any work lost during those afternoon hours will be made up when those employees return to work well-rested and highly motivated.

> The teacher is the single most important factor affecting student achievement.
>
> The principal is the single most important factor affecting building culture.
>
> #TurningPoints

■ ■ ■

Allowing teachers to leave early on the last day of work may seem insignificant. But in a profession with few perks, school leaders must look for every opportunity to show employees they are valued.

Recommended Reading:
Education

In addition to the books already referenced in *Turning Points*, below are fifteen more *education* titles to add to your reading list. While not exhaustive, these resources provide a good starting point for anyone wanting to dig deeper into the educational philosophies shared in these pages.

Books are arranged alphabetically by author.

‣ *The Art of Coaching*, by Elena Aguilar

‣ *Because of a Teacher,* by George Couros

‣ *The Flat World and Education*, by Linda Darling-Hammond

‣ *Mindset,* by Carol Dweck

‣ *Grit*, by Angela Duckworth

‣ *The Leader's Guide to Unconscious Bias,* by Pamela Fuller

‣ *Leading Change,* by John Kotter

‣ *Road to Awesome,* by Darrin Peppard

‣ *Drive,* by Daniel Pink

‣ *Evolving with Gratitude,* by Lainie Rowell

‣ *Street Data,* by Shane Safir

‣ *Lead from Where You Are,* by Joe Sanfelippo

‣ *Educated,* by Tara Westover

‣ *What Great Teachers Do Differently,* by Todd Whitaker

‣ *The Principled Principal,* by Jeff Zoul and Anthony McConnell

For more book ideas, visit *www.drjaredsmith.com/book-summaries*

PERSONAL GROWTH

"If you're serious about changing your life, you'll find a way. If not, you'll find an excuse."[1]

—FROM *You Are a Badass*
BY JEN SINCERO

THE PURSUIT OF HAPPINESS

"When I have a car, I'll finally be happy!"
"When I go to college, I'll finally be happy!"
"When I get a girlfriend, I'll finally be happy!"
"When I buy a house, I'll finally be happy!"
"When I am a principal, I'll finally be happy!"
"When I earn my PhD, I'll finally be happy!"
"When I get married, I'll finally be happy!"
"When I write a book, I'll finally be happy!"

These have been my thoughts throughout life. I assume when a certain milestone is reached, life will be complete.

Each goal listed above has been achieved. And while clearing each hurdle produced brief bursts of enjoyment . . . those moments were short lived.

I'm not alone in my thinking. We assume when we get a promotion, date the right person, make more money—life will be good. Yet, in most cases, we return to our natural level of well-being shortly after reaching our destination.

This begs the question: *Why does true happiness feel so fleeting?*

First Car: Nothing better than rolling around in the
1990 Ford Tempo blasting some Nelly!

■ ■ ■

One my favorite books about the psychology of happiness is *Happier* by Tal Ben-Shahar. In his book, Ben-Shahar outlines four distinct happiness *archetypes*, which are default attitudes toward happiness that all humans possess. Those archetypes are *Hedonism, Rat Race, Nihilism,* and *Happiness.*[2]

While Ben-Shahar's research is outstanding, his terminology is a bit academic. To assist with comprehension, I've translated his archetypes into four happiness *"mindsets":*

Self-Indulgence Mindset: Do you focus on immediate pleasure while completely ignoring the future consequences of your actions? True accomplishment takes time, yet humans are conditioned to forego future benefits in exchange for quick hits of satisfaction in the form of objects, food, activities, and entertainment. Like Veruca Salt in the classic *"I want it now!"* scene from *Willy Wonka & the Chocolate Factory,* today's instant gratification culture reinforces the hedonist mindset.

Rat-Race Mindset: Do you choose to suffer during the present for the purpose of anticipated gains in the future? Many people believe true happiness is found later in life, only after decades of hard work and sacrifice. Rather than be thankful for what we already have, society tells us that personal contentment comes only after we have accumulated more money, power, and possessions than our peers.

Woe-Is-Me Mindset: Do you struggle enjoying the present moment while also lacking a sense of future purpose? If *self-indulgence* describes living in the present, and *rat-race* describes living for the future, *woe-is-me* describes living in the past. Rather than believe they control their destiny, many people stubbornly blame past circumstances for their lack of personal and professional advancement.

Fulfillment Mindset: Do you participate in activities that bring you present enjoyment while also leading to a fulfilling future? To feel optimal levels of happiness, people should identify and engage in actions that provide both *present enjoyment* and *future gains.* According to Ben-Shahar, people who embed these activities into their daily and weekly routines live the happiest lives.

To be clear, constant happiness through the *"fulfillment mindset"* is impossible as not every activity can provide present enjoyment and future benefit. Sometimes we must focus on the present—such as taking a day off from work to rejuvenate our mind. Alternately, sometimes we must focus on the future—such as skipping a night out with friends to complete a graduate class assignment.

Also, understand these are mindsets—*not actual people.* To varying degrees, we all possess characteristics of all four mindsets. For example, many educational leaders (myself included) get stuck in the rat race mindset: *"When I reach the next level of leadership—I'll finally be happy!"* they say. However, three months into their "dream job," they discover their general happiness is no different than before.

■ ■ ■

"I already know what makes me happy," some readers may be thinking. *"I don't need to change anything!"*

Unfortunately, humans are bad at predicting future happiness. In *Stumbling on Happiness*, Daniel Gilbert suggests that we are bad at predicting our future emotional states because we rarely reflect on the emotions that accompany recent experiences.[3] Whereas we assume a particular activity will produce happiness, these predictions are often inaccurate.

For example, people regularly associate passive relaxation with happiness. *"I can't wait to lay around and do nothing on Saturday!"* is a statement we have all made. However—after a day of laying on the couch, watching television, eating junk food, and scrolling through our phones—we often feel fatigued and anxious as opposed to refreshed and peaceful.

Another common mistake is overestimating the enjoyment of a special event. *"New Year's Eve is going to be epic!"* people predict as they plan an evening of fine dining and limitless cocktails. While some experiences meet expectations, in many cases NYE ends up being a huge letdown. Combine spending too much money with a terrible hangover . . . and we are likely to feel *worse* on January 1st than most days of the year!

Alternately, say you are part of a community organization. In these clubs, you are often asked to volunteer time to assist with local projects. When the sign-up form reaches your table, you smile at the sheet while secretly thinking, *"How am I going to get out of this without looking like a jerk?"* Little do we realize that volunteering is one activity that produces the highest levels of happiness.[4]

Finally, recall the concept of *adaptation* (see page 62). Adaptation is a psychological phenomenon wherein humans quickly return to their default level of happiness despite experiencing significantly positive life events. Studies have found that after an initial burst of happiness, lottery winners report feeling no happier than before winning the jackpot. A similar phenomenon happens when people buy "stuff." Thinking they will *"finally be happy"* after buying a new house, car, wardrobe, or accessory, people quickly return to their baseline levels of happiness a short time later.

So how do we identify the specific actions that will bring us true happiness? Here are four ideas to consider:

Reflect: Given that feelings of happiness depend on the individual, careful attention must be given to the feelings produced by everyday actions. Use a notebook or electronic document to record your daily tasks and evaluate them according to how happy each makes you feel. Devoting a few minutes to this practice when your memory is fresh will provide valuable insight into your preferences for genuine enjoyment.

Daily Gratitudes: One surefire method for improving happiness is keeping a daily gratitude journal. Each night before bed, write down at least three things for which you are grateful. Examples could be as small as the morning sunrise or as big as a relationship with a spouse. While writing your ideas, consider the feeling each detail brings. What emotions are associated with these items? Focusing on positives before bed not only leads to better rest, it increases the likelihood that life's bright spots are remembered.

House Money: The term *"playing with house money"* is a psychological phenomenon where gambling one's winnings (typically at casinos) feels less risky than gambling the money that was brought from the outside. In education, a similar phenomenon happens when teachers realize they don't have to work because a snow day has been called. During these unexpected days off, small pleasures—such as sipping on coffee or reading a book— are magnified and trivial anxieties vanish. Training your brain to approach each day as a "snow day" can create optimal levels of happiness.

Fulfillment Mindset: In *Atomic Habits,* James Clear suggests that we *"engage in actions that contribute toward our desired identity."* [5] When I read this line back in 2018, I couldn't help but think about all the time I was wasting: *"Does scrolling through social media and watching sports really make me happy?"* I wondered. When I replaced those trivial activities with more meaningful work—such as reading and writing—my happiness skyrocketed while my anxiety decreased (more on this in the next chapter). I have found that *investing in myself* is one of the best ways to embrace Ben-Shahar's fulfillment mindset.

My ex-wife didn't leave much when she moved out . . . but she did leave this sign. Was she trying to tell me something?

■ ■ ■

When I get a promotion, I will have peace.
When I make enough money, I will relax.
When I have more power, I will be content.

We have all made these comments.

However, I challenge you to do this: Imagine going back five years ago and being told you would have all of the "things" that you have today: the job, the possessions, the money, the relationships. Odds are, you would be insanely jealous of your future self.

Although prolonged bliss often feels elusive, understanding the psychology of happiness—and identifying our personal conditions for joy—helps us get one step closer to living a fulfilling life.

LIVING WITH ANXIETY

During my first day of work as a teacher in the Chicago Public Schools in 2007, all 60 faculty members gathered in the auditorium.

As is typical of many opening day meetings, employees were asked to stand up and introduce themselves by sharing their name and professional background.

Being seated toward the back of the auditorium, I was one of the last people to speak. One by one, staff shared their information. As the introductions worked their way up and down the rows, I began feeling something I had never felt before: *intense anxiety.*

With each passing introduction, I felt my heartbeat escalate. By the time introductions made it to my row, my heart felt like it was going to pound itself right out of my chest. *"What the hell is going on?"* I thought as my Navy blue Ralph Lauren polo shirt jumped off my chest with every pulse.

As the person next to me got up to speak, I felt my throat tighten—to the point where it was difficult to breathe. The room was spinning, sounds were amplified, and it was nearly impossible to process what was happening.

Finally, it was my turn to speak. Shaking uncontrollably, I stood up and mumbled, *"Jared . . . Smith"* loud enough for only the people closest to me to hear. Unable to concentrate, I looked at my new colleagues with a blank stare.

I stood still for a few more seconds, hoping to say something coherent. However, the pressure in my head was so extreme and the ringing in my ears so intense that talking was impossible.

Unsure what to do next, I returned to my seat.

The person next to me hesitated for a moment before standing up to share her information. Even so, I could feel all eyes on me. *"Who is this new guy?"* I imagined my new colleagues thinking. *"And why is he so weird?"*

Once the introductions made their way to the final row, I darted into the hallway, found the closest bathroom, and locked myself in a stall where I hid for the next 30 minutes until we were dismissed to our classrooms.

■ ■ ■

For the next five years, I continued to have panic attacks any time I was asked to introduce myself or share information in a public setting. Too afraid to admit something was wrong—and deathly afraid to come off as incompetent to my peers—I developed escape plans which would get me out of these situations. Whether it was "accidentally" showing up late to avoid formal introductions—or taking an "emergency" phone call to sidestep public speaking—I developed methods to avoid situations triggering my anxiety.

My school picture from 2007—please ignore the obnoxious "diamond" earring.

However, I soon realized this approach was unsustainable. If I had any hope of moving up the administrative ranks and fulfilling my limitless potential, I needed help. So, in 2012, I set up an appointment with a general physician to share my concerns.

As the appointment started, I was incredibly embarrassed about my condition. I didn't want to admit I was a "head case" to anyone, let alone someone I had never met before. However, my mood quickly changed when the doctor assured me that my experiences were quite common. He explained that people deal with panic attacks for a variety of reasons, and that medicine could mitigate these situations.

Beyond panic attacks, the doctor determined that I had a mild form of generalized anxiety disorder. *"Oh man, I really am crazy,"* I thought upon hearing the diagnosis. However, the doctor again calmed my fears by not only prescribing medication, but also by telling me that my situation was very common.

I felt a sense of relief upon leaving the doctor's office. Understanding my experiences were completely normal and that help was on the way did wonders for my mental health, and served as a turning point in my battle with anxiety.

■ ■ ■

Anxiety disorders are the most common mental illness in the United States. According to the US Department of Health & Human Services, there are five types of anxiety disorders:

Generalized Anxiety Disorder is chronic anxiety and exaggerated worry about everyday life events (such as work, relationships, and finances) for no obvious reason.

Obsessive-Compulsive Disorder (OCD) consists of recurrent, unwanted thoughts (obsessions) and/or repetitive behaviors (compulsions) that significantly interfere with a person's daily activities.

Panic Disorder is characterized by unexpected and repeated episodes of intense fear accompanied by symptoms such as a racing heart, shortness of breath, dizziness, and chest pain.

Posttraumatic Stress Disorder (PTSD) develops after experiencing or witnessing a terrifying event that results in flashbacks, nightmares, and severe anxiety about the incident.

Social Anxiety Disorder can be described as extreme fear and anxiety in social settings that interferes with relationships, daily routines, work, school, and other activities.[6]

It is estimated that 60 million American adults—one-third of the adult population—have an anxiety disorder.[7] And while today's health providers offer patients a host of therapy and medication options, nearly 25 million American adults (40% of those with an anxiety disorder) go without help. And while a small number of adults genuinely lack access to treatment, most adults simply refuse to ask for assistance.

In a world where we are conditioned to visit a doctor for the smallest of concerns, why do so many people refuse to ask for help with anxiety?

Two words: *Denial* & *Stigma*

After experiencing my first panic attack, I refused to admit I had an issue. *"I drank too much coffee,"* I reasoned. So, when the next panic attack happened without caffeine, blame shifted to workout supplements: *"I really need to lay off the Creatine!"* With each passing panic attack, new excuses were formed.

It took dozens of panic attacks to admit I had a mental health issue. And while I was willing to share my story with a few family members, the last thing I wanted was to seek treatment: *"I'm a successful person—not a head case,"* I argued. *"I can handle this on my own."*

Truth is, I was embarrassed about the mental illness stigma. For people who are used to high levels of success, admitting that you have mental health issues seems counterintuitive and can be viewed as a sign of weakness.

■ ■ ■

My anxiety issues can be traced back to early adolescence. And while I haven't quite solved the anxiety riddle (job interviews and hangovers are my kryptonite!), three decades of learning, testing, and reflecting has allowed me to keep my anxiety in check.

Here are seven of my best ideas for dealing with mild to moderate anxiety:

We're In This Together: Jerry Seinfeld—the most decorated comedian of our lifetime—has been vocal about his battles with mental illness. In a recent interview, Seinfeld shared that anxiety *"always seems to accompany those who have high levels of creativity."* [8] Hearing these words helped me normalize my struggles. Understanding that Seinfeld and several other highly-talented individuals (e.g., Oprah Winfrey, Johnny Depp, Taylor Swift, Michael Phelps) all deal with mental illness gives me comfort in knowing I'm not alone.

Share Your Story: Being open with staff about my mental health issues has been a complete game changer. Not only do employees appreciate my vulnerability, those individuals with their own mental health concerns feel good knowing that I understand their situation. To be clear, I'm not running around yelling *"Look at me—I have anxiety!"* but rather I search for timely opportunities to discuss this topic. Finally, I have found great power in openly sharing my story with students: *"Wow Dr. Smith, I had no clue we are so alike!"* is a common response from kids who have their own mental health issues.

Medication: People have mixed feelings about taking medication. Personally, I believe that physical activity and a healthy diet eliminates the need for most prescriptions. But anxiety is a different beast. While I'm not sure if it's the medication or if it's the placebo effect . . . I would highly recommend that anyone with chronic anxiety take medication. Currently, I take 40mg of Celexa (citalopram) daily. Also, I take Xanax (alprazolam) when my anxiety is at its worst—usually only a couple times a year.

Journal: When I go through periods of high anxiety, I find comfort in journaling. One thing I often write about is how—in the moment—whatever I am worried about seems like such a big deal. *"My anxiety is high because I do not want to face this issue,"* is a fairly common journal entry. However, when looking back on those comments months later, I realize how exaggerated those worries really were. Understanding that human beings are remarkably bad at predicting how various experiences make them feel long-term has helped reduce my anxiety.

Mindfulness: The root cause of my anxiety is often rumination, meaning I'm in my bed tossing and turning at 2:00am while my mind replays something that happened in the past (such as a missed opportunity or an ended relationship) or forecasts what could happen in the future (such as an unpleasant conversation or losing my job). In these moments, it's incredibly helpful to have mindfulness tricks to stop my mind from wandering. One of the easiest tactics is counting out long breaths (*inhale . . . exhale*) while blocking out all other thoughts. Can you make it to ten? It's harder than you think!

Social Media: It should be no coincidence the sudden rise in mental health problems has coincided with the explosion of social media. Anyone dealing with anxiety should consider uninstalling phone apps (e.g., Facebook, Instagram, Twitter) that can be accessed via laptop. Not having these apps at your fingertips may leave you bored (*"Gasp—what will I do with my free time?!"*) but your anxiety gets a much-needed break. Not ready to delete apps? At the very least, turn off notifications.

Workout: Exercise is an absolute no-brainer for anyone dealing with anxiety. Physical activity kicks up endorphin levels, the body's famous "feel good" chemical that produces feelings of happiness. Whereas I shoot for 45 minutes a day, even 30 minutes 3 times a week is a great place to start. Looking for a quick win? Rather than watch *another* episode of *Parks and Rec*, go for a walk outdoors. Your mental health will love you!

■ ■ ■

"But Jared, I don't have any issues with anxiety. Why should I care?"

Even if you don't have anxiety, it is likely that one-third of your employees do, meaning school leaders must be empathetic of staff who deal with anxiety-related issues.

Have you ever asked a teacher to share an idea in a room full of staff, only to have them turn down your request? *"What do you mean you don't want to speak in front of your colleagues?"* you may have thought. *"You speak in front of kids all day!"* Understand that anxiety is triggered in different ways . . . some of which do not make logical sense.

Also, don't forget about students. Anxiety and depression have been identified by students as the biggest problem facing teenagers—ahead of bullying, drugs, alcohol, and gangs.[9]

Tell me if you've heard this one before: *"What do you mean you don't want to give a presentation?"* some teachers ask their students. *"Well, I guess you'll just take a zero!"* Students must be given the benefit of the doubt with anxiety-related issues. Rather than force students to act or behave a certain way, schools must adjust to meet the needs of students with mental health concerns.

In short, school leaders must view every situation through a lens of compassion—not compliance.

> School leaders must view every situation through a lens of compassion—not compliance.
>
> #TurningPoints

■ ■ ■

I share my battle with anxiety not to make anyone feel bad for me, but rather to empower readers who may be going through similar experiences. Chances are, some of you reading this chapter are thinking, *"Holy crap—he is talking about me!"* If this is the case, don't hesitate to reach out and share your story.

Anxiety can be hugely debilitating and prevent highly talented people from reaching their full potential.

Don't let this be you.

Understand that you are not alone, and that millions of others are going through similar experiences.

To-Do or Not To-Do

As a beginning school administrator, I thought I had everything figured out. Rather than commit to lifelong learning and implement "best practices," I flew by the seat of my pants and trusted natural ability to guide my work.

Growing up, I had always relied on memory to keep track of tasks needing completion. And given that follow-through never seemed to be an issue, I didn't think a formal process for tracking daily commitments was necessary.

Quite often, I would see other administrators carry notebooks where to-do lists were kept. Upon seeing their lists, I would tell them: *"Wow, that's really cool. I need to do that!"* while in my head I was thinking, *"Wow, that's really lame. I will never do that!"*

As a stubborn new administrator, keeping a to-do list was the *last* thing I wanted to do (pun intended). To-do lists weren't sexy or innovative; they reminded me of grocery shopping at *Hy-Vee* with my mom as a child.

As an assistant principal, I got away with my memory-based system. Whereas occasionally I would forget to return a parent phone call, conference with a student, or send an important email . . . for the most part I was pretty dependable.

Everything changed when I became a head principal. Whereas previously I managed a group of 30 to 40 employees, I suddenly found myself the boss of 200-plus individuals.

Throughout the day, staff would approach me from all directions with various requests. Given my desire to be helpful, these conversations usually ended with me agreeing to help the employee. Whereas initially I managed to stay up-to-speed with my promises, over time commitments started falling through the cracks.

Upon realizing I had dropped the ball on a promise, employees would say, *"Oh don't worry—you have a lot going on."* Despite these kind words, I couldn't help but detect their disappointment. Furthermore, I noticed these employees stopped coming to me for assistance.

My story is common in educational leadership: Many administrators fail to follow through on commitments to staff in a timely manner. Even worse, many leaders forget their commitments all together.

And when this happens—rather than apologize to the employee and seek ways to improve—these leaders justify their actions by saying, *"I'm just so swamped right now,"* *"I have a lot on my plate,"* and—more recently—*"We're just so short-handed."*

Unfortunately, these leaders fail to understand the following leadership truth:

Few things kill trust faster than a boss who doesn't follow through.

> Few things kill trust faster than a boss who doesn't follow through.
>
> #TurningPoints

■ ■ ■

At the start of the day, school leaders have mountains of tasks to complete. Meetings, observations, reports, phone calls, emails . . . the list is endless!

Unfortunately, administrators have a bad habit of arriving at the office, opening their laptop, and starting work without a clear list of priorities. When this happens, they spend their day haphazardly jumping from one task to the next without a clear sense of direction.

Enter the good old-fashioned to-do list.

Studies have shown that people perform better when they have systems for keeping track of commitments. To-do lists provide structure and organize priorities. Not only does having a trusted system for capturing thoughts reduce anxiety, crossing items off lists produces bursts of motivation and positivity.

Countless resources provide guidance on capturing commitments. Two of my favorites are the *Getting Things Done* method and the *Bullet Journal Method.*

David Allen is recognized as one of the leading experts on personal and organizational productivity. In his book *Getting Things Done*, Allen suggests the following:

> *Studies have demonstrated that our mental processes are hampered by the burden put on the mind to keep track of things we're committed to finish, without a trusted plan or system in place to handle them. . . . Every idea you have of something that needs to get done must be captured somewhere outside of your head.*[10]

Ryder Carroll has garnered recent attention for the *Bullet Journal Method*. In his book with the same name, Carroll shares this advice:

> *Holding on to thoughts (as opposed to writing them down) is like trying to catch fish with your bare hands: They easily slip from your grasp and disappear back into the muddy depths of your mind. Writing things down allows us to capture our thoughts and examine them in the light of day. Each item we write down begins to declutter our mind. We're creating a mental inventory of all the choices consuming our attention.*[11]

Whether leaders explore one of these methods or develop their own process does not matter. What does matter is that leaders must stop relying on memory and develop a system for capturing commitments.

■ ■ ■

Looking to improve your follow-through on commitments? Consider these six ideas:

Moleskine Notebooks: I always carry a small notebook so I can document my commitments and revisit my to-do list at any time. Writing down commitments in "real time" not only eliminates the possibility of the task being forgotten . . . it also decreases the underlying anxiety caused by not remembering what needs to be done. Although they have a funny name, *Moleskine Notebooks* are among the most popular in the industry. I prefer the 5" x 8.25" version with the hard cover. I also love my *Pilot G-2 07* pens.

Weekly Routine: Each Monday morning I spend a few minutes listing every professional and personal commitment on one page in my notebook. Incomplete tasks from the previous week get transferred, while new obligations from the weekend get added. Throughout the week, I add new duties the moment they come up. And when finished, I take pleasure in crossing off the task (more on this to come). The page serves as my weekly playbook.

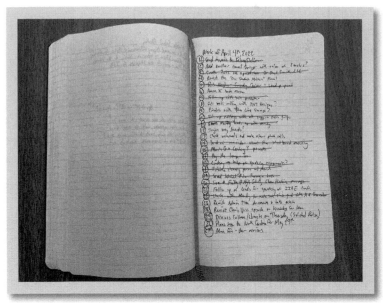

Using a Moleskine notebook to capture commitments has been a game changer.

Pictures Are Worth a Thousand Words: In 2012, I saw a student use her cell phone to take a picture of the whiteboard in a math classroom. The picture—which contained a number of formulas—would be used for the student's future reference. At the time I thought, *"That's weird . . . and not for me."* Now I have found that taking pictures is one of my most efficient strategies for remembering tasks needing my attention. Taking five seconds to snap a photo saves me precious time and allows me to revisit the picture whenever my mind needs a refresher.

Circle Back: Keeping promises not only builds trust with employees, it creates a culture of high expectations. With this in mind, I recommend that supervisors look for opportunities to inform staff when tasks have been completed . . . even when it feels like the communication may not be necessary. Letting them know when a task is complete—such as meeting with a student or calling back a parent—not only shows employees they are valued, it sends a message to staff they are also expected to follow through on their own commitments.

Cross Off: Do you get a strange sense of excitement when crossing off your to-do list? It's not just you, research shows that checking items off of a checklist makes us happier, less stressed, and more productive. Looking for another psychological advantage? During an especially "unproductive" day or week, flip through your notebook pages and notice how many obligations have already been done. Seeing hundreds of crossed-off items feels therapeutic and helps suppress pessimistic thoughts.

Increased Accountability: In addition to following through on their personal commitments, one of a leader's most important jobs is to ensure that employees follow through on their own commitments. To help keep my employees accountable, I create a Google Doc for each direct report. Within this shared document, I keep track of commitments that are made during our weekly 1:1 meetings. Without this system in place, it would be nearly impossible to hold double-digit direct reports accountable to their various commitments.

▨ ▨ ▨

In *Keep Going*, Austin Kleon suggests the following:

> *Whenever I need to figure out my life, I make my list. A list gets all your ideas out of your head and clears the mental space so you're actually able to do something about them. When I'm overwhelmed, I fall back on the old-fashioned to-do list. I make a big list of everything that needs to get done, I pick the most pressing thing to do, and I do it.*[12]

Do you find it difficult to address your biggest priorities?
Do you find it challenging to hold employees accountable?
Do you find it hard to stay upright in the daily whirlwind?

Look no further than the good old-fashioned to-do list.

Warning: Nerd Alert!

"The person who stops studying merely because they have finished school is forever hopelessly doomed to mediocrity, no matter what their calling. The way of success is the way of continuous pursuit of knowledge."[13]

—FROM *Think and Grow Rich*
BY NAPOLEON HILL

■ ■ ■

When asked about their goals in life, most people provide similar answers:

We want gratifying jobs and fulfilling careers.
We want healthy bodies and strong minds.
We want meaningful relationships and loving families.
We want sufficient resources and financial security.

Whereas these goals sound fairly basic, many people struggle to make their dreams a reality. One recent study found that roughly 70% of people fail to achieve their personal goals . . . and that doesn't include the 80% of people who never set goals in the first place![14]

Similar to navigating downtown Chicago without a GPS (damn you Lower Wacker Drive!), many people set goals without having a clear sense of how to actually *reach* those goals.

For those who are driven to make the most out of life, I've got great news for you: *The blueprint for achieving the life of your dreams is already written down somewhere waiting to be discovered.*

■ ■ ■

If you think I've always enjoyed reading, you're wrong.

I used to *detest* reading.

Here is the *full list* of assigned books I read from cover to cover starting in 7th grade:

Middle School: *The Westing Game*
High School: *Of Mice and Men*
College: *Harry Potter and the Sorcerer's Stone*
Master's: *None*

That's right. I read *3 books* in nearly 12 years of formal education. *"Reading is a waste of time,"* I insisted.

It wasn't until my 27th birthday when I finally discovered the power of reading. During my family birthday party at Texas Roadhouse, my dad gifted me the previously mentioned *Total Money Makeover* by Dave Ramsey (see page 78). Initially, I wasn't thrilled about the present. *"A book? What a waste!"* I thought to myself as I politely smiled and showed the book to family members.

However—when I opened the book a few months later—I couldn't believe how much helpful information was stored in one place. At this point in life I had accumulated a credit card bill of nearly $20,000. Mistakenly thinking that I was *"building credit"* and *"doing what all Americans do,"* I quickly realized that my spending philosophy was terribly misguided.

Rather than watch another episode of *The Real World: Cancun* or reorganize my Top 8 Friends on Myspace, I found myself devouring *The Total Money Makeover* while trying to learn more about personal finance. The knowledge I gained from Ramsey's book was a major turning point in my life, as I follow many of his financial principles to this day.

Another shift in my attitude toward reading happened in 2012 when I read *What Great Principals Do Differently* by Todd Whitaker. At this point, I was in my fifth year as an assistant principal. Although I didn't mind being an AP, I had been turned down for several head principal jobs . . . which had me second-guessing my leadership abilities.

Whitaker's book came at the perfect time. Not only did I pick up several new ideas, the book also confirmed many of my thoughts about educational leadership. Countless times while reading I found myself thinking, *"That's what I do! I knew that was right!"* These realizations restored my professional confidence and convinced me to focus on what I could control, as the right opportunity would eventually come.

Eventually, I realized for all of life's challenges—from public speaking to physical fitness to personal branding—a template for success had already been created. It was now up to me to find these resources and consume the information.

In *The Five Major Pieces to the Life Puzzle,* Jim Rohn echoes these thoughts:

All of the books that we will ever need to make us as rich, as healthy, as happy, as powerful, as sophisticated, and as successful as we want to be have already been written. The question is: In the last ninety days . . . how many books have we read?[15]

Unfortunately, leisure reading in America is at an all-time low. According to the Bureau of Labor Statistics, only 19% of Americans read for leisure.[16] Furthermore, the average American reads 17 minutes a day, which pales in comparison to the amount of time spent on social media (127 minutes), watching television (120 minutes), and checking email (94 minutes).

"But my life is already crazy busy," you might be thinking. *"And I waste very little time."*

I get that we all have busy lives. In addition to our professional responsibilities, many of us have spouses to spend time with, kids to care for, and countless other competing priorities. I understand that setting aside large chunks of time for reading is not feasible for everyone.

However, understand that many of the problems that consume our daily thoughts—such as money problems or work relationships—have already been solved *and* explained. By investing a little time to read (and implement) this information, we could save ourselves a lot of time (and heartache) in the long run.

■ ■ ■

I love learning about the reading habits of others (*nerd alert!*). Not only do I pick up new ideas, I find inspiration when I realize others use similar approaches.

To help inspire your reading habits, below are eight reading "principles" I follow:

What Books Do You Buy? My book-buying rule is simple: *If you're thinking about getting a book, buy it.* Lifelong learners must approach a $25 book as though it has the potential to change their life. Don't think of books as a cost . . . think of books as an *investment.* It is fairly common for me to spend upwards of $2,000 a year on books.

My home office is littered with nonfiction books.

Print Book vs. Ebook vs. Audiobook? Call me old-school, but I prefer reading print books over the more modern options. The purpose of reading nonfiction books should be to retain information and put ideas into practice. Print books allow me to quickly take notes and mark sections to revisit. To be clear—*any reading is better than no reading*—so choose the option that works best for you.

How Many Books Do You Read a Year? I read about 30 books per year. But rather than focus on a "book count," my goal is to read 30 minutes per day. A lot of readers get consumed with the number of books read, making it hard for them to quit a book they have already started. Using a *quality over quantity* mindset gives readers permission to quit a book that provides little value.

How Many Books Do You Read at a Time? I typically read between three to five books at a time. Having options allows me to select the book that matches my current mood. If I'm sick of thinking about leadership, I'll switch to a motivational self-help book. If my workouts are feeling lethargic, I'll pick up a book on fitness or dieting. There's really no rhyme or reason to which book I read at a given point, I simply allow inspiration to guide me.

How Do You Take Notes? I have a unique—but efficient—format for note-taking that I call the *"slash/bracket"* format. When I'm reading a book and come across a section that I want to revisit at a later time, I put brackets around the section and put a slash at the top corner of that page. Being able to quickly leaf through books and revisit key points allows me to retain information while reading several books at once.

What Do You Do When You Finish a Book? Once a book is finished, I revisit all of the pages with slashes to determine if the bracketed information is helpful. The notes that are most impactful make it into a book summary that is posted on my website. Finally, all notes are dumped into a master spreadsheet where they are organized by theme. Having the passages organized this way allows me to easily revisit key ideas when trying to solve a problem or look for inspiration.

Do You Reread Books? Yes! Rereading books can be incredibly powerful. People who come back to a book after a long break

---

PERMISSION TO BE GREAT

and micromanagement from leadership are some of the recent trends that threaten educator autonomy and contribute to burnout. Simply stated, one way to promote engagement is to allow educators more control and autonomy.

Encouragement, Recognition, and Appreciation (ERA)

I love baseball and throughout this book you will encounter a few stories related to this passion of mine. In baseball, a lower earned run average (or ERA) is a good thing, as this is an indicator of the number of runs for which a pitcher is responsible and a reliable statistic to measure pitching performance. When referring to school leadership, it is exactly the opposite and best to have as high an ERA (Encouragement, Recognition, and Appreciation) as possible. Encouragement, recognition, and appreciation includes the financial and social acknowledgement one receives for contributions on the job consistent with expectations. Examples of ERA include praise, awards, supportive feedback, perks, acknowledgement, and salary. These examples are designed to recognize and reinforce positive behavior. While financial compensation is necessary and awards are nice, research from Chapman and White (2019) has shown that the everyday appreciation workers receive is even more valuable. The number one factor in job satisfaction is not the amount of pay received, but whether people feel appreciated and valued for the work they do. On the other hand, when encouragement, recognition, and appreciation are absent, as in Maria's situation, there is a strong likelihood of an employee heading down the road to disengagement, burnout, and inefficacy. People want to be acknowledged and know that what they think, say, and do matters. As you work through the content of this book, you will discover a multitude of examples designed to boost ERA in the school setting.

The slash/bracket note-taking method is great for retention.

often discover new insights that were previously missed. Why? Because perspectives change over time. When I come back to the same book a couple years later, I often can't believe the quality content that was missed the first time around.

Do You Ever Hit a Wall? For a variety of reasons, we all go through reading dry spells, myself included. When this happens, I've found I'm able to get back into the groove by rereading something that has really spoken to me in the past. Instead of expecting a random book to get me out of my funk, I choose a book from my list of favorites.

■ ■ ■

In *The 7 Habits of Highly Effective People*, Stephen Covey shares the following:

> *There's no better way to inform and expand your mind on a regular basis than to get into the habit of reading good literature—you can get into the best minds that are now or have ever been in the world.*[17]

The blueprint for achieving the life of your dreams has already been created.

You just need to read it.

Be Like Mike

Michael Jordan is widely considered the greatest basketball player of all time. In his 15 seasons in the NBA, Jordan won six NBA titles and was named league MVP five times. In 1999, ESPN named Jordan the "Top North American Athlete of the 20th Century."

Tim Grover was Michael Jordan's personal trainer. During their years together, Grover had the unique opportunity to see what made Jordan so successful. While he was blessed with remarkable talent and generational athleticism, Grover believed Jordan's *strict discipline* and *daily routine* is what set him apart from his peers. *"MJ had the most disciplined game-day routine I've ever seen,"* Grover said in his book *W1nning*. He went on to state:

> *He planned and organized every detail of his day, from the time of his workout to the car he drove to the arena. He put his clothes on in a specific order, organized the game tickets for his family and friends, ate at the same time every day . . . everything had purpose and discipline.*
>
> *Why was routine so important to him? Because the games themselves were so unpredictable. And controlling the unpredictable was his specialty. His routine allowed him the mental freedom*

and clarity to focus on one thing: the complexity of the game, and managing every variable that stood between himself and a win.[18]

**What kid growing up in the 90s didn't have
an MJ poster on their bedroom wall?**

■ ■ ■

"So, Michael Jordan was super disciplined and followed a precise routine," you may be thinking. *"What does that have to do with me?"*

Many parallels can be drawn between the contests played on the NBA hardwood and the jobs we complete as school leaders. Basketball games—much like school days—are unpredictable. Similar to how basketball teams must change their game plan as a result of foul trouble to a key player or the hot shooting of the other team, school leaders must change their game plan due to the behavior incident of a student or the effects of severe weather.

Discipline allows leaders to stay focused in the midst of the "daily whirlwind" that defines school leadership. In schools, it's easy to get caught up in external factors affecting the workday. Whether those incidents are as minor as a staff member not showing up to work or as major as dealing with the COVID pandemic, leaders are counted on to steer the ship when the waters get choppy.

But what does discipline look like in the work setting? As discussed in *Learning Curve*, effective leaders identify high-leverage activities that can be executed on a daily basis—regardless of how crazy the day gets.

On *The Group Project Podcast* I interviewed Melissa Barlow. Barlow is a high school principal just outside of Oklahoma City and was named the 2020 Oklahoma High School Principal of the Year. With more than 2,600 students and nearly 200 staff members, Barlow leads one of the largest schools in Oklahoma.

Given the number of people Barlow is responsible for on a daily basis, one might assume her day resembles a game of *Whack-A-Mole* at Chuck E. Cheese. However, Barlow was quick to identify *discipline* and *routine* as key factors helping her stay focused in the midst of chaos:

> *"The day can get away from you. It's crazy!"* Barlow said. *"As administrators, you're going to get pulled in a million different directions. For me, it's about scheduling and knowing that what's on my calendar is important. There are times when things come up such as student discipline or a parent showing up to talk to you . . . but it's really important that I prioritize meeting with staff.*

> *"I do a lot of touch-base meetings,"* Barlow continued. *"I really believe that it's important to get those meetings on your calendar.*

All those meetings are preplanned in the summer. After I greet the kids in the morning and the bell rings for first hour, I'm looking at my schedule for the day. A lot of my time is spent meeting with staff and building relationships.

What gets scheduled gets done."

Whereas Barlow prioritizes "touch-base" meetings with staff, others may identify different daily actions that have the greatest impact on school outcomes. Whether the focus is classroom walkthroughs, student relationships, or academic interventions is irrelevant; what's important is that leaders are disciplined about executing those activities regardless of what the day might bring.

▦ ▦ ▦

"But being disciplined is soooo boring," some people may be thinking. *"Who wants to do the same routine every day?"*

Certainly, society has programmed us to believe that self-discipline is lame:

"You always eat so healthy . . . live a little!"
"You're going to bed at 9? It's the weekend!"
"Do you really need to work out every day?"
"Why are you saving for a car? Get a loan!"
"Don't you ever take a day off from work?"

Whereas social norms tell us that it's "cool" to be spontaneous, research indicates that discipline and success are interconnected. Not only do people who prioritize discipline and routine generate more income, have healthier bodies, experience less anxiety, and attain personal goals . . . they are also more likely to enjoy happier lives.[19]

"Happiness?" you may be wondering. *"Following a daily routine does not sound like fun."*

Certainly, *discipline* and *happiness* seem to be two contradicting concepts. Discipline feels like "hard work" while happiness is associated with "not working." Whereas the absence of work may result in momentary gratification, replacing self-discipline with self-indulgence ultimately results in negative feelings.

As previously discussed (see page 188), one of the biggest mistakes people make is predicting how "downtime" makes them feel. When asked what the perfect Saturday looks like, at one time all of us have responded, *"I just want to lay on the couch, watch my favorite shows, eat a bunch of snacks . . . and do nothing!"*

While the thought of binging YouTube videos and crushing Krispy Kreme donuts sounds amazing . . . have you ever noticed your mood at the end of these days? Whereas most people believe a day free from discipline and routine will make them feel peaceful, cheerful, and rejuvenated, most people end up feeling agitated, grumpy, and sluggish.

Another example is vacation. When planning trips, the question of whether or not to continue daily routines (workouts, sleep times, eating habits, etc.) often comes up. Whereas sleeping in and being a beach bum all day sounds tempting (dos piña coladas, por favor!), ambitious individuals often report feeling agitated and anxious when routines are completely abandoned.

That's not to say we don't need time to relax and rejuvenate. All humans have a limited *"cognitive bandwidth,"* meaning that our brains can only handle so much work each day. At some point, we must give our minds a rest by completing activities that recharge our batteries.

Several chapters of this book were edited while vacationing in Cancún.

However, the next time you abandon all routine and discipline for a day, reflect on your levels of happiness; you might be surprised how the "perfect day" really makes you feel.

■ ■ ■

Discipline and routine are proven to positively impact many aspects of life. In addition to professional practice, they are key ingredients to physical fitness, dieting, personal growth, relationships, personal finance, hobbies, and other life endeavors.

While discipline and routine are simple concepts, they are difficult to execute. Here are five ideas to consider:

Remove Temptations: Self-discipline is often easiest by following an *"out of sight, out of mind"* mentality. Removing distraction is crucial for implementing discipline and routine into your daily schedule. Want to read a book but can't stop looking at your phone? *Turn off the phone.* Want to lose a few pounds but can't stop eating Hot Cheetos? *Stop buying junk food.* Want to move on from an ex but can't stop looking at their photos? *Block them on social media.* Want to save money but can't stop making Amazon purchases? *Cancel your Prime membership.*

Wake-Up Call: When we were kids, we loved weekends. Why? *We got to stay up late and sleep in!* Unfortunately, adults wanting to add more discipline to their life will want to resist their inner child by establishing a routine where they consistently go to bed and wake up at the same times . . . even on the weekends. As we age, our bodies struggle to adjust to major shifts in sleep schedules. Even slight changes—such as staying up an hour later than usual—can affect memory, alertness, and immune systems for days.[20]

Celebrate: Even the most disciplined people must build in celebrations to salvage their mental health. For the longest time, I was ultramethodical around fitness and dieting; I lifted weights every day and ate healthy at every meal. Although I was jacked . . .

I wasn't happy. I have learned to build in minicelebrations—no lifting Fridays and cheat meal Saturdays—to give my mind a much needed break. *"Those don't sound like celebrations,"* you may be thinking. Incidentally, people who prioritize discipline find great pleasure in activities that others consider commonplace.

Say No: When days are organized around top priorities, it becomes easier to say "no" to requests that may take us away from those goals. Similar to Melissa Barlow's story earlier in the chapter, I also prioritize meeting with staff throughout the week. For each direct report (usually around ten employees), I hold a 30-minute 1:1 meeting at set times throughout the week. Because those meetings are already on the calendar, it becomes much easier to say "no" to other, less important requests that come my way.

You're Crazy: People who embrace a routine-based lifestyle must understand they will be labeled as "boring" and criticized by their peers. As was mentioned earlier, those who practice self-discipline are in the minority and are oftentimes ridiculed by others in our instant-gratification culture. So, when you eat salad instead of

> To be in the top 1% in your space, you must be willing to do what 99% of people are unwilling to do.
>
> This mindset will result in others thinking you're crazy. When this happens, remember that hard work is the price of greatness.
>
> #TurningPoints

ordering Dominos with your colleagues—or go to bed early as opposed to throwing down a few Busch Lights (or White Claws) with your friends—be prepared to be mocked by others.

■ ■ ■

In 1991, Gatorade launched the *"Be Like Mike"* advertisement campaign. In these television commercials, children of various ages were shown imitating Michael Jordan's most recognizable basketball moves. For readers alive during the MJ era, you can probably recall the *"Like Mike, if I could be like Mike"* jingle in your head.

Ironically—three decades later—I've come to realize the deeper meaning to this memorable marketing campaign.

Whereas I used to mimic Jordan's moves on the court (with tongue out, obviously), I now find that his mindset *off* the court is what I most want to imitate.

FOUNTAIN OF YOUTH

One day in 2013, my buddy Monterio and I were lifting weights at the gym.

During this particular workout, Monterio and I had low energy and weren't lifting as much as usual. So—like normal guys—we blamed the poor showing on "getting old."

"Man, my back is sore!" Monterio complained after finishing an underwhelming set of bench press.

"I hear you," I responded after completing my own lackluster set. *"My body has been stiff all day!"*

"You know our bodies fall apart at 26," my 24-year-old lifting partner suggested as he reracked the weights.

"What!? I just turned 31!" I replied. *"That means I'm waaaay past my prime?"*

"Yeah, bro. It's all downhill from here."

Those were *not* the words I wanted to hear. As someone who found motivation by being "fit," I didn't like that my biological clock was already ticking and there was nothing I could do to stop it.

Monterio and I "up in da club" in 2013.

For the next few years, every time my body had a minor setback, I remembered Monterio's ominous words.

Knee hurting after a run? *"There you go—old age!"*
Legs stiff from sitting all day? *"I'm turning into my dad!"*
Neck sore from sleeping wrong? *"You're falling apart!"*

Despite these minor setbacks, I stayed focused on living healthy. Beyond lifting weights, I continued to soak up information about physical activity and clean dieting. New ideas turned into miniexperiments to see what worked. While some ideas were quickly discarded, other suggestions produced positive results. The concepts that stuck around would turn into my *healthy-lifestyle philosophy*—a set of principles that guide my everyday decisions.

I recently turned the big 4–0. While I'm not happy about the increase in white hairs and unflattering wrinkles (can we please start filtering school pictures?), I'm happy to share that my friend's prediction of my physical downfall was overblown. Not only does my body feel great, I would argue that my physique is as good as ever.

My experience has led to the following realization:

Body aging is inevitable.
Body decay is optional.

■ ■ ■

Today we find ourselves facing an unprecedented health-care crisis.

Despite living in a world with more exercise programs, weight-loss products, and dieting options than ever before, more than two-thirds of all Americans are obese. As society continues to normalize sedentary behavior and promote unhealthy eating, we live in a culture that *encourages* weight gain.

To be clear, there's much more to physical fitness than looking good in a swimsuit.

Consider that 70% of premature deaths—heart attacks, strokes, diabetes, and other illnesses—are caused by factors *within our control.* But rather than address the root cause of these concerns with exercise and dieting, most adults turn to *medication* as the solution to their health issues. Americans spend nearly $200 billion annually on obesity-related medication, which translates to overweight couples paying almost $4,000 more in health-care costs per year as compared to their normal-weight peers.

"What you're saying makes sense," you may be thinking. *"But at the end of the day, I'm just too exhausted to work out or worry about my diet."*

While adding exercise and dieting to an already busy day may sound exhausting, that's looking at it backward. We are not tired because we exercise too much . . . *we are tired because we don't exercise enough.* Countless studies have shown that regular exercise and healthy eating increases energy and reduces fatigue. In fact, any work time that is "lost" due to working out or eating a healthy lunch is more than compensated for thanks to an increase in workplace productivity.

Unfortunately, unwritten "rules" in the educational workplace do us no favors. Consider the way educators treat lunch. In many school districts, uninterrupted lunch breaks are abnormal. Rather than take 30 minutes to recharge their batteries, studies suggest approximately 50% of teachers are expected to supervise students while eating lunch. Furthermore, nearly 20% of educators skip lunch altogether.[21]

School leaders also experience the lunch-break dilemma. Administrators who take a lunch are often viewed as selfish or lazy. *"You're taking . . . a lunch break?"* teammates question, as if their colleague is committing an unspeakable crime. This "I'm-not-doing-my-job-if-I-take-a-lunch" mentality results in many school leaders skipping lunch out of guilt. And for those who do eat, many do so while supervising the cafeteria or checking email.

Besides eating lunch, working out is often looked down upon in our profession. Despite recent advancements in promoting healthy lifestyles, schools still house a harmful undercurrent that discourages making time for self-care. *"How do you have time to work out?"* teammates question the "fit" teacher on the team, as if she is not committed to her job. *"Between grading and planning, I don't have any extra time."*

The same goes for school leaders. When telling others that I work out every morning from 6:45am–7:30am, I often get confused looks and backhanded compliments: *"Man, I wish I had time to exercise,"* some leaders will say. *"But I need to be at work. My people expect me to be there."*

Similar to how society encourages weight gain and normalizes sedentary behavior, so too does the unspoken culture in the educational workplace.

■ ■ ■

At this point, some readers are rolling their eyes.

"You've obviously been in great shape your whole life. You don't know what I'm going through."

Those who read *Learning Curve* understand that I have experienced my fair share of physical and emotional ailments.

As a college student, I went from an in-shape, 180-pound high school senior to an out-of-shape, 220-pound college senior. Thanks to late-night Papa John's and all-you-can-drink jungle juice (is this still a thing?), I was headed down the wrong path.

Furthermore, as was previously discussed (see page 193), in my mid-20s I developed severe anxiety issues related to panic attacks. Not understanding what was happening and too embarrassed to say anything, I lived with these symptoms for years without telling anyone or going to a doctor for help.

Finally, in my 30s I developed ulcerative colitis. Similar to Crohn's disease and other inflammatory bowel diseases, ulcerative colitis is an ailment that impacts 1% of Americans and causes inflammation and sores—called ulcers—in the lining of the rectum and colon.

With each setback, I had every reason to fall off the wagon and let my body "go." But thanks to understanding the long-term implications of healthy living, I overcame these bumps in the road.

"Oh, cry me a river! Please don't try to convince me to diet or exercise. I'm doing just fine. Plus, my wife says she likes my dad bod."

Unfortunately, this is the mindset that plagues many adults. In our 30s, 40s, and 50s, the sedentary lifestyle may not result in noticeable side effects. But, in the long run, very few people can overcome a lifetime of inactivity. Consider this quote from *Younger Next Year* by Chris Crowley and Henry Lodge:

> *A lot of people unconsciously assume that they will get old and die: one phrase, almost one word, and certainly one seamless concept. That when they get old, they will die soon after, so a deteriorating quality of life does not matter. That is a deeply mistaken idea and a dangerous plan for your life. In fact, you will probably get old and live. You can get decrepit, but you are not likely to die; you are likely to live like that for a long, long time.*[22]

■ ■ ■

Me in 2018 (off the wagon) versus me in 2022 (on the wagon).

The following are ten principles that outline my *healthy-lifestyle philosophy*. Please understand that we all have different bodies and physical fitness goals. While many of these ideas have universal application, you will want to experiment to find the combination of ideas that works best for you.

Less is More: Understand that *exercise is the single, greatest key to keeping your body from completely falling apart.* But how much time is needed? When I was younger, I used to think anything less than a 60-minute workout was a waste. However, I discovered that spending hours at the gym led to frequent injuries and lingering soreness. Not good when you're in your 20s! Now I believe that *30 to 45 minutes per day* is all you need to be in great shape.

Workout Plan: There are *thousands* of ideas on what makes the "ideal" workout. Whether you go for a hike at a nearby park— or attend a spin class at your local gym—doesn't necessarily matter. What does matter is that your heart rate is elevated for a sustained period of time. My typical workout is 20 minutes of cardio and 20 minutes of lifting weights. My lifting is normally done using *supersets*—performing multiple exercises back-to-back with short rests in between . . . perfect for keeping the heart rate going. More on this in the following chapter.

Feel the Burn: Raising your heart rate is important because high-intensity workouts lead to significant caloric burn throughout the rest of the day. Known as the *afterburn effect,* research shows that vigorous exercise increases metabolism and burns calories for up to 24 hours . . . meaning people who exercise actually *lose weight* during the day. Want better news? The calories shed during afterburn are often those stubborn fat calories in our midsections (men) and butt/thighs (women). Talk about a win-win!

Engage Your Core: Your body's core is made up of your lower back to your abs and everything in between. Because they are at the center of every movement, we must keep these muscles strong and limber. Engaging your core—squeezing your core muscles into a tightened position while still breathing normally—is one of the most underrated practices for an optimal workout. While remembering to "flex" your core while exercising can be difficult, forming this habit not only limits nagging back injuries, it is the secret sauce for getting six-pack abs.

Walk This Way: I used to hate walking. *"Walking is for my grandma!"* I thought while hopping on the treadmill and cranking it up to 9.0 mph. However—over time—my thinking has changed. Not only is it easy on your joints, walking is a great way to promote creative thought; some of my best ideas have come while walking. While it's not going to burn calories like running or other high-intensity cardio, many great thinkers and leaders have found walking to be their most enjoyable—and productive—daily routine.

Calories Matter: When I was younger, I tried many "fad diets." From Atkins (severely limiting carbohydrate intake), to Slow Carb (choosing from a limited list of foods), to the Egg Diet (my personal creation—would not recommend), I've tried everything to drop weight and lose fat. However, I've since learned that every controlled weight-loss study has essentially concluded the following: *If you consistently consume fewer calories than you burn, you'll lose weight.* Understanding this simple rule and focusing on a target daily calorie count has helped me meet my fitness goals. More on this in the following chapter.

Avoid Grazing: Teachers lounges and school offices are notorious for being stocked with goodies. From potluck leftovers to day-old donuts, unhealthy food is always available. While limiting snacks—a cookie here and a handful of chips there—is a great start, understand that calories add up over time. Say you grab a small snack (200 calories worth) each day. In isolation, these calories are negligible. But when snacking happens every other day, that's an extra 36,000 calories per year. Given that a pound of fat is roughly 3,500 calories, this totals 10 extra pounds of fat. *Sheeeesh* (said in a high-pitched voice, obviously).

Scenes like this are found in teachers' lounges all across the country.

Be Careful: In my late 20s, I followed a super-strict diet where I ate "clean" all the time. However, one night I was going crazy thinking about food, so I went to Little Caesars and crushed a supreme deep dish and an order of Crazy Bread. An hour later, I felt so bad about "all the weight I gained" that I went for a 60-minute run. Warning: *Trying to have a perfect diet at all times is a ticket to the mental ward.* Whereas you should avoid eating bad stuff all the time, you can certainly let loose every so often and be fine. In fact, research shows that the most long-term weight gained from a single cheat meal is only a few ounces.

Measure Progress: Before cell phone cameras, I relied on the scale to track my body composition progress. However, several factors—such as daily weight fluctuations and scale inaccuracies—complicated those measurements. Now I believe that *mirror selfies* (yes, you read that right) are best for measuring progress. I know . . . taking underwear pics when you are in your 40s, 50s, and 60s seems a little childish. However, I've found that flipping through several months' worth of progress photos provides me with the motivation to continue my fitness journey.

Give it Time: We live in the *Age of Impatience.* People want 24 workweeks, 6-minute abs, and 30-second meals. I hate to break it to you, but don't believe those IG fitness models who claim you can get Hugh Jackman's arms or Carrie Underwood's legs in a week. Transforming your body is extremely rewarding, but it's a slow process. Trade the dream of overnight success for slow, measured growth. It's going to be a grind before people take notice. But once you start hearing *"Wow, you look amazing"* and *"Geez, you have really slimmed down"* you will realize the hard work is paying off.

■ ■ ■

Beautiful things happen when you commit to a healthy lifestyle and refuse to let your body decay.

Just imagine living a few extra decades—and staying ultrafit as well.

Whereas others are confined to assisted-living beds due to a lifetime of sedentary behavior, you will be traveling with your spouse, spending time with grandchildren, and living your best life.

RIPPED:
GET FIT AT ANY AGE

Whereas the previous chapter outlined ten general principles for healthy living, this chapter provides a comprehensive overview of the *diet plans* and *workout routines* I have used to stay in great shape at 40 years old.

Please understand that this chapter is much longer than most chapters in this book. However, I am so convinced of the positive correlation between physical fitness, professional success, and general well-being that I felt compelled to empty my entire playbook.

"But what do you know?" you might be thinking. *"You're not a trained professional!"*

You're right. I'm not a trained professional. Nor do I claim to have everything figured out.

However, I have spent the better part of *two decades* reading, writing, listening, and learning about fitness. I enjoy experimenting with new ideas, tracking how my body responds, and adjusting for optimal performance.

Whereas I may not have the "personal trainer" title, very few people have given physical fitness as much attention as me.

Given my profession, I decided a shirtless pic would not be wise.

■ ■ ■

Getting ripped begins—and ends—with a healthy diet. No matter how hard you work out, if your intensity toward dieting does not match your intensity toward exercise, it is impossible to get shredded.

Getting ripped begins—and ends—with a healthy diet.

No matter how hard you work out, if your intensity toward dieting does not match your intensity toward exercise, it is impossible to get shredded.

#TurningPoints

"Dieting is so overwhelming," you may be thinking. *"I don't even know where to start!"*

I don't blame you.

Every time we look, a new fad diet is sweeping the country. Atkins, South Beach, Vegan, Keto, Paleo . . . there are too many to choose from! And now with Instagram "models" and TikTok "influencers" constantly shoving diet ideas down our throats, it's impossible to know who to believe.

Do not get suckered into buying these products and plans. Instead, understand that weight loss is simply *calories consumed* versus *calories burned.* In fact, every weight-loss study conducted over the past century has concluded *if you consistently consume fewer calories than you burn, you'll lose weight.*

Consuming fewer calories than are burned is commonly referred to as a *calorie deficit diet*. The first step in a calorie deficit diet is determining your *daily calorie target*—the number of calories you must stay under to lose weight. While there are several methods for calculating your daily calorie target, the most accurate is the Harris-Benedict Formula.

Several online calculators for the Harris-Benedict Formula exist. My current favorite can be found at inchcalculator.com /harris-benedict-calculator. When using this calculator, you will be asked to enter your age, gender, height, weight, and activity level. Below were my numbers at 40 years old:

Harris-Benedict Calculator (TDEE & BMR)

Calculate TDEE & BMR using the Harris-Benedict equation.

Age: 40

Gender: ● male ○ female

Height: 75 [in ▾]

Weight: 180 [lb ▾]

Activity Level: heavy physical exercise 5-6 times per week ▾

CALCULATE

Your Total Daily Energy Expenditure (TDEE):

3,225 calories/day

Activity Level	Calories
Basal Metabolic Rate (BMR)	1,869
little to no exercise	2,243
light exercise 1-3 times per week	2,570
moderate exercise 3-5 times per week	2,897
heavy physical exercise 5-6 times per week	3,225
heavy physical exercise 6-7 times per week	3,552

Daily energy expenditures for various levels of activity.

I want to highlight two things about this table: the *Basal Metabolic Rate* (BMR) and *Total Daily Energy Expenditure* (TDEE).

BMR is the number of calories naturally burned each day based on age, gender, height, and weight. My BMR is 1,869 . . . meaning if I never left the house and lived a sedentary lifestyle, I would need to consume less than 1,869 calories per day to lose weight. While this number is realistic, I would *not* recommend a life of inactivity (more on this later).

TDEE is the number of calories naturally burned (BMR) *plus* the calories that are burned as a result of physical activity throughout the day. My TDEE is 3,225 calories, meaning I can consume nearly 1,400 more calories per day and still maintain or lose weight thanks to having an active lifestyle.

When using the Harris-Benedict Formula, keep in mind the following:

Eat less calories than your TDEE = *lose* weight
Eat the same calories as your TDEE = *maintain* weight
Eat more calories than your TDEE = *gain* weight

One important rule of thumb to know is *there are roughly 3,500 calories in a pound of fat.* This means if you cut 3,500 calories from your diet (or burn 3,500 calories through exercise), you can expect to lose a pound of fat.

For example, say your TDEE is 3,000 calories and you only eat 2,000 calories a day. Given our rule (3,500 calories = 1 pound of fat), how much weight can you expect to lose in a week?

3,000 TDEE – 2,000 calories consumed = 1,000 daily calorie deficit
1,000 daily calorie deficit x 7 days = 7,000 calories "under" TDEE
7,000 calories/3,500 (one pound of fat) = **2 pounds burned in one week**

Once a daily calorie target has been determined, you must develop a system for tracking the number of calories consumed throughout the day.

"But Jared, isn't calorie counting bad?"

I get it. The words "calorie deficit" and "calorie counting" have endured plenty of criticism, especially as the number of mental health issues related to dieting continues to climb.[23] However, most people have no idea how many calories they consume. In fact, most adults dramatically underestimate their calorie intake—often by as much as 2,000 calories per day.[24]

So, how does one calorie count? One of the best places to start is the *MyFitnessPal app*. MyFitnessPal has a massive database containing the calorie and nutrient data for thousands of foods. Whenever you consume any food or drink, simply enter your items and the app does the math for you.

At first, I didn't think I needed to count calories. *"This is a waste of time,"* I thought as I reluctantly tracked calories using MyFitnessPal for the first time. However—at the end of the first day—I couldn't believe my eyes. I had consumed well over 4,000 calories! No wonder I wasn't losing weight.

From that day forward, I used the MyFitnessPal app to track every meal, snack, drink, and dessert for several months. At first, it was hard to take 1,000-plus calories out of my daily diet. *"What do you mean I can't have a bowl of ice cream after dinner?"* I pouted. However—over time—my appetite got used to the new normal.

After several months of tracking hundreds of meals and individual food items, I no longer needed the MyFitnessPal app because I had memorized the calories for the handful of foods I ate regularly. And for the foods I didn't eat regularly, I developed a ballpark idea of their calorie amounts.

This brings me to a key idea for this chapter: *Having a general understanding of the calorie counts for most common foods is a valuable skill to learn.* Those who follow a calorie deficit diet don't always have the time to track calories. Therefore, it is important to learn how to do quick mental math to ensure your daily calorie target is not exceeded.

■ ■ ■

One common calorie-counting question has to do with food quality: Does nutrition matter? Or, is it all about the calories?

Mixed opinions exist on this topic. Some people maintain that calories are all that matter. This means you could eat 13 S'mores Pop Tarts (2,405 calories) or 4 Big Macs and a medium Coke (2,462 calories) and still lose weight assuming the daily calorie target is preserved.

While I haven't tried living off of Pop Tarts or Big Macs, I have read enough to know that people who want optimal results should eat a well-balanced diet full of foods that are rich in vitamins, minerals, and other nutrients.

This is where a personal rule of thumb comes into play called *the 80% Rule.*

The 80% Rule suggests people who are serious about weight control should eat "clean" foods 80% of the time. Eating clean means choosing foods that are close to their natural state and not overly processed. Clean foods are typically found around the perimeter of a grocery store and include fresh fruits, vegetables, lean meats, whole grains, and dairy products.

For the other 20% of the time, people are allowed to eat "non-clean" food. Nonclean foods are typically found in the center of the grocery store and include heavily processed and prepackaged foods such as chips, cookies, cereals, breads, frozen dinners, soda, and alcohol.

In a moment I will propose that unhealthy eating should be limited to one "cheat" day per week. People who follow this model eat clean six out of seven days a week—or 86% of the time. No matter if you use the "cheat day" approach or a different system, eating clean 80% of the time is a great rule of thumb to follow.

■ ■ ■

Are you ready for a sample meal plan?

Recall my numbers from earlier in the chapter: 40 years old, male, 75 inches tall, 180 pounds and a TDEE of roughly 3,200 calories per day. Given that I am still trying to lose that last bit of fat—plus I have a built-in cheat day (more on this later)—**my current daily calorie target is 2,500 calories.**

The following is the meal plan I have used for the last couple years. I usually follow this meal plan Monday through Friday, with a "Cheat Day" on Saturday, and a slightly modified—yet healthy—day on Sunday.

Please note that these measurements and nutritional facts are simply *estimates*. I encourage you to adjust the amounts based on personal preference:

Morning Preworkout

1 packet *Super Orange Emergen-C*
1 scoop *Fruit Punch No-Xplode*
1 cup ice
Mix with 10 ounces water

Total = 65 Calories

▪ ▪ ▪

Breakfast: Dr. J's "Famous" Breakfast Smoothie

½ cup vanilla Greek yogurt
1 cup frozen blueberries
1 cup spinach
1 ½ cup original, unsweetened almond milk
1 scoop *Cinnamon Crunch Quest Protein Powder*
1 tsp. cinnamon
¼ cup rolled oats
Blend in Ninja blender for 60 seconds

Breakfast Total = 500 Calories and 30g Protein

▪ ▪ ▪

Lunch: Dr. J's "Power-Lunch" Omelet

3 egg whites and 1 egg (cooked omelet style)
½ cup mushrooms
1 cup spinach
½ cup peppers
½ cup onions
4 thin slices deli turkey

4 thin slices deli ham
Side: one large handful of almonds
Side: ½ cup 2% cottage cheese
Drink: 20 oz water

Lunch Total = 700 Calories and 35g Protein

■ ■ ■

Afternoon "Wake-Me-Up" Drink

1 packet *Raspberry Emergen-C*
1 scoop *Fruit Punch No-Xplode*
1 cup ice
Mix with 10 ounces water

Total = 65 Calories

■ ■ ■

Dinner: Dr. J's "Incredible" Egg Sandwich

½ bagel (sliced and toasted)
3 eggs (cooked omelet style)
3 thin slices deli turkey
3 thin slices deli ham
½ ounce shredded cheese
Side: one large handful of almonds
Drink: 20 oz water

Dinner Total = 725 Calories and 35g Protein

■ ■ ■

Dessert: Dr. J's "Soooo Good" Protein Smoothie

1 scoop *Cookies & Cream Quest Protein Powder*
2 tbsp. *PB2 Powdered Peanut Butter*
¾ cup original, unsweetened almond milk
1 cup ice
Blend in Ninja blender for 60 seconds

Dessert Total = 175 Calories and 30g Protein

DAILY TOTAL = 2,230 CALORIES AND 130g PROTEIN

The "incredible" egg sandwich; I've eaten this dinner hundreds of times the past few years!

This diet plan often raises questions. Here are a few of the most common:

"You eat the same meals Monday through Friday? Lame!"

I realize that most people do not want to eat the same foods every day. However, consider the foods you currently eat on a daily basis. I'm willing to bet you eat a lot of the same foods regularly—especially for breakfast and lunch. Fact is, most people tend to rotate through a number of "staple" meals throughout the week. Once you find meals that are tasty and healthy, I would suggest that you rotate through those meals for the sake of convenience and to prevent overeating.

"My spouse will never go for this!"

I agree, most spouses will not appreciate the rigidity of this plan. When I was married, my wife loved to cook for us. Of course, I knew better than to turn down her homemade meals! To compromise, I would eat my "typical" breakfast (500 calories) and lunch (700 calories), but then at dinner I would eat whatever my wife had made. Knowing that I had roughly 1,000 calories to play with gave me plenty of options, yet helped prevent overeating (and resist dessert!).

"Wait, you make omelets for lunch? Aren't you supposed to be at work?"

When I moved into my first superintendent role, I bought a house within walking distance of my office. While initially hesitant about the location, I loved being so close because I could go home for lunch. I'll be honest . . . my head is *spinning* by the time the noon hour rolls around. Rather than continue to scramble my mind by eating lunch at my desk, I run home to decompress and eat a healthy meal. Any time lost by taking a lunch break is more than made up for, thanks to increased afternoon productivity. School leaders wanting to perform at the highest levels would be wise to schedule daily mental health breaks.

"How did you choose those foods?"

I have spent years researching the best foods to eat. Depending on the study, you can make a case that *any* food is good for you (*"Drink red wine and eat dark chocolate and you'll live to be 110!"*). Most foods on my meal plan are selected not only because I like the taste, but also because they are proven to burn fat.

Consider the following:

Why Almonds? While nuts contain more calories per gram than most foods, they are natural dietary fats that also boost metabolism. Studies indicate that participants who eat almonds with meals lose more body fat and more stomach fat compared to groups who don't eat almonds.

Why Blueberries? Blueberries have been shown to speed up the fat-burning process and are protective against weight gain. Furthermore, eating three servings of blueberries per week has proven to reduce heart attacks by as much as 34%.

Why Eggs? Few foods contain proper nutrients while also managing hunger like eggs. Regardless of how you like yours cooked (I'll take mine over hard, please), eggs are proven to speed up fat loss and reduce food cravings throughout the day.

Why Mushrooms? Mushrooms are an excellent source of fiber, which enhances weight loss. Other nutrients like potassium, copper, and B vitamins support cognitive functioning. Adding two to four servings of mushrooms per week helps improve memory and reduce cognitive impairment by nearly 50%.

Why Spinach? Just like Popeye the Sailor Man, humans gain incredible powers from this low-calorie, leafy vegetable loaded with nutrients. Not only is spinach great for weight loss, this superfood also strengthens bones, improves eyesight, and enhances skin quality.

"I'm strong to the finish 'cause I eats me spinach."

Why Water? Drinking large amounts of water increases metabolism and triggers the release of stored body fat. Drinking 20 ounces of water within a couple minutes temporarily boosts metabolism rates by 30% and burns around 25 calories. While 25 calories may not seem significant—when done three times a day over the course of a year—27,375 calories (more than seven pounds of fat!) are burned.

■ ■ ■

"OK, so tell me about your cheat days."

Before we discuss my cheat day, let's be clear that eating disorders are nothing to mess with. Many people who participate in strict diets have problems with bulimia and anorexia. If you experience mental health issues related to dieting, please contact a health professional.

To combat potential mental health issues, it is important to build in diet breaks. A cheat day is when you have one opportunity each week to splurge on all your favorite foods. By giving yourself permission to eat pizza, French fries, donuts, cookies, ice cream, and all of your guilty pleasures, bottled-up cravings are removed from your system, so you can focus on eating healthy for the remainder of the week.

Psychologists and nutritionists agree that cheat meals allow individuals to eat better throughout the week.[25] This planned calorie splurge allows people to forgo other unplanned and binge-inducing meals—meals that take much longer to recover from and could throw you off the wagon altogether. Furthermore, research shows cheat meals increase metabolism, causing you to burn calories faster.

"But I gain five pounds on cheat days! Aren't I ruining my diet?"

Many people worry they've "blown" their diets after a single instance of overeating. What they don't realize is any weight gained is mostly water weight. In fact, the most fat anyone can gain from a single meal or day—no matter how much they've eaten—ranges from a few ounces (after a cheat meal) to one pound (after a cheat day).

I've discovered that any added weight after Saturday's cheat day is normally gone midweek. And if I have two or three cheat days in a row (such as with a holiday or vacation), the weight is usually gone in seven to ten days. Of course, this assumes you return to your diet after the cheat day (or days) are done.

■ ■ ■

"So how do you approach your cheat day?"

Arguably, Saturday is the perfect cheat day due to the countless temptations pulling you from your diet. Whether you are out of town with family, at a football game with friends, or at the farmers' market with your spouse . . . choosing Saturday as a cheat day allows you to eat (and drink) whatever you want without hesitation.

Below is a pretty standard cheat day: For simplicity, this meal plan assumes I'm at home on a Saturday. In most cases, my cheat days are split into *Morning* (cheat day lite) and *Evening* (cheat day heavy):

Breakfast (Cheat Day Lite)

One packet *Maple Pancakes Oats Overnight*
One packet *Strawberries & Cream Oats Overnight*
Mix 1/2 cup original, unsweetened almond milk per packet
Warm in microwave for 2 minutes

Breakfast Total: 600 Calories and 50g Protein

■ ■ ■

Lunch (Cheat Day Lite)

1 box *Kraft Macaroni & Cheese*
1 can tuna
1 large handful of almonds
1 *Chocolate Peanut Butter Fit Crunch Protein Bar*
Mix tuna into fully prepared macaroni

Lunch Total: 1700 Calories and 80g Protein

Dinner (Cheat Day Heavy)

4 cups *Dot's Pretzels*
2 cups *Peanut M&M's*
4 *Chocolate Chip Lovers Toll House Cookies*
4 slices *Casey's Supreme Pizza*
1 pint *Ben & Jerry's The Tonight Dough* ice cream
2 20 oz bottles of *Diet Pepsi*
There is no correct order for eating these items

Cheat Dinner Total: 4,000 Calories and 60g Protein

CHEAT DAY TOTAL: 6,300 CALORIES AND 190G PROTEIN

■ ■ ■

Now that you have the diet down, let's discuss working out.

In the following paragraphs, I detail my overarching workout philosophies, along with a sample workout plan to follow.

Please understand that these ideas are meant for individuals who have a baseline knowledge of exercise. Rather than spend time explaining each lift in detail, you are encouraged to perform a quick Google or YouTube search for help.

Recall that exercise is the single, greatest key to keeping our bodies from completely falling apart as we grow older. Despite having more workout and gym options than ever before, only one in four adults exercises regularly.

Around age 32, the default signal in our body flips over to decay. Every year—for the rest of our life—we get weaker, our metabolism slows, and our body becomes less coordinated. As depressing as it sounds, there is nothing we can do to reverse the effects of aging. But what we can do is significantly slow down the aging process . . . by staying physically active.

"But Jared, I'm a busy school leader! And I have a family. I just don't have the time to work out."

I get it. Most people don't think they have enough time to exercise. When you look at all of the things school leaders are expected to do, working out often falls low on the list of the priorities.

However, take a closer look at how your time is spent. Please understand there is a huge difference between *being busy* and *being productive*. Whereas many people believe they have no room in their daily schedule for exercise, upon closer examination they spend a lot of time on frivolous activities such as scrolling through social media and watching television.

Listen, we're not talking about spending hours at the gym. Instead, we're talking about 30 to 45 minutes a day. When you consider those minutes make up roughly 3% of a 24-hour day . . . this hardly seems like an absurd ask considering exercise's countless benefits.

"Ok, so what do you do in those 30–45 minutes?"

I'm glad you asked. The following is a quick overview of how I structure my workouts which include a combination of walking, lifting, rowing, and stretching:

Monday: 20 min walk/20 min lift
Tuesday: 20 min walk/20 min lift
Wednesday: 20 min walk/15 min row
Thursday: 20 min walk/20 min lift
Friday: 20 min walk/20 min stretch
Saturday: 20 min walk/20 min lift
Sunday: 30–45 min walk

You probably noticed that every day begins with a walk. *"Walking, that's not much of a workout!"* you may be thinking.

A few years ago, I would have agreed with you. I have always assumed "cardio" meant crushing an intense run, pounding out a fast-paced elliptical session, or beasting the stair step machine.

However, I now realize the toll those activities take on my body. And even more important, those activities are hard on me *mentally*. This brings me to one of my biggest realizations about working out: the key to consistency is finding activities that your body can handle and that your mind enjoys.

Which brings us back to walking.

In the past, I used to run a lot. I mean like *19-minute 5Ks* and *90-minute half-marathons* lot.

I would run three hard miles before lifting weights. While I was burning calories like crazy, I wasn't building muscle. Then I realized that all of that running was counterproductive against my *real goal*, which was to look like Brad Pitt in *Fight Club*.

Over time, I began to realize the power of walking. Walking is ideal because calories are burned without stifling the process of growing muscle. Walking is also proven to get people in the *fat-burning zone*—a place where fat is burned, but muscle is preserved.[26]

Equally as important, walking is great for mental health. Walking gives me an opportunity to disconnect from the stresses and pressure of work, and shift my focus on thoughts that are positive and uplifting. It's not just me; studies show that people who walk regularly experience elevated moods of happiness.

To help maintain a positive mindset, I have one rule of thumb for walking: *Do not scroll through social media.* Have you ever looked around at a busy gym to see what others are doing while on cardio machines? That's right—they're aimlessly browsing through social media feeds. Do not fall into this trap. Rather than get jealous of others (*how did he land that girlfriend?*) and experience FOMO (*how was I not invited on this trip?*), use your walk as a time to focus on yourself.

Nothing like a 20-minute walk to get the mind right and the blood flowing.

One of my best tricks for productive walks is to watch inspiring YouTube videos. Most recently, I've been watching concerts and live music of my favorite artists. There is something hugely motivating about seeing musicians at the top of their game, putting on a show for thousands of people. These videos pump me up and give me the chills!

Another thing I like to do is bring a book to read. I'm not a Kindle person, so this typically involves bringing a physical book with me. While I haven't quite figured out the best system for reading and walking . . . it feels great knowing that I am doing something productive with my body *and* my mind.

Finally, while walking I try to go at a pace of 3.0 to 4.0 miles per hour with a slight incline of 1 to 3 percent. These settings help get my heart rate up so I'm ready for my lift, without beating up my body.

■ ■ ■

Once the 20-minute walk is done, it's time to start lifting. Similar to walking, my thoughts on lifting have shifted dramatically over the years. Growing up in the 90s, I was taught the following:

Focus on one muscle group per day
Complete three sets of ten "reps" per lift
Take 60 seconds of rest between sets

However, my views toward lifting changed when I took a "boot camp" class in my early 30s. In that class, we lifted heavy weights and were always supersetting—performing multiple exercises back-to-back with short rests in between—while also hitting many muscle groups (chest, arms, legs, shoulders, etc.) throughout the session.

This boot camp approach was a turning point in my lifting philosophy for three reasons. First, I realized it was okay to hit multiple muscle groups per day. Second, I realized you could get a great full body workout in less than 30 minutes. Third, I realized "cardio" could be accomplished while lifting by simply taking less rest time between exercises.

Although I no longer attend these classes, I have adopted a boot-camp mentality with my workouts. Whenever possible, I superset full body lifts with heavier weights while limiting the rest time between sets.

Before we look at a sample workout plan using these principles, let's address a few questions:

"You say 'full body lifts'—what do you mean?"

My workouts center around these four core lifts: squats, deadlifts, bench press, and power clean and press. They are called "full body" lifts for a reason; when you do these lifts you are hitting dozens—if not *hundreds*—of different muscles all over the body. Not only is this an efficient way to lift weights, these lifts also provide a great foundation of strength for your body. In addition, I always look to insert two great bodyweight exercises—push-ups and chin-ups—into my workouts. Eighty to ninety percent of my lifts focus on these six exercises, or a variation of these exercises.

"How many reps do you go for?"

One of my favorite fitness books is *Bigger Leaner Stronger* by Michael Matthews. Matthews contends to build muscle, you should shoot for six repetitions (reps) of each movement per set. If you can do six or more reps, you should go up in weight. If you can do four or five reps, you're at the correct weight. If you can only do three reps or less, you should go down in weight.[27]

This approach encourages the use of heavier weights and pushes lifters to increase weights when possible. This has proven to be a simple—yet effective—rule of thumb for lifting.

"How do you choose your lifts? Do you have a rotation?"

First, I avoid doing the same exercises two days in a row. Endless research suggests muscles must be given at least a 48-hour break for recovery. Beyond that one tip, I don't have a weekly rotation. Thanks to years of lifting, I am able to select from a menu of exercises at a moment's notice. Rather than follow a specific rotation, my lifting choices usually depend on how my body is feeling (skipping body groups that are sore) and what equipment is available (some dudes love to hog squat racks).

"What about ab exercises? I want my six-pack to show!"

Listen, folks: *ab-specific exercises are not necessary.* Rather than waste your time doing thousands of crunches, get in a habit of constantly squeezing or "flexing" your abdominal and lower back muscles while doing full-body workouts. Furthermore, abs don't show until body-fat percentages reach certain points (12% for men and 18% for women) . . . meaning six-pack abs are the result of a healthy diet and regular exercise, *not* side planks and flutter kicks.

"But what about arms? I want killer biceps!"

Go to any gym and you'll see people standing in front of the mirror doing endless bicep curls. Similar to abdominals, I have found the secret to defined arms (both biceps and triceps) is focusing on full-body lifts. Sure, you can spend hours working on your arms and probably get similar results . . . *but you are a busy school leader!* Instead, save yourself time and get the sculpted arms you want by using the boot camp approach outlined on the previous pages.

■ ■ ■

Below is a sample daily workout plan. However, recall that my days are fluid and driven more by how my body feels and what equipment is available as opposed to any one routine.

Prior to completing the following workouts, start with a 20-minute walk at a rate of 3.0 to 4.0 miles per hour with a slight incline. Exercises should be completed consecutively for a total of 5 to 6 supersets. Take 20 to 30 seconds of rest between each exercise (and set). Shoot for 6 reps unless otherwise noted.

Monday Lift (20 Minutes)

Barbell Squats
Dumbbell Curl into Shoulder Press
Push-ups (15–20)

Tuesday Lift (20 Minutes)

Barbell Deadlift
Dips (10–15) or Skull Crushers
Myotatic Crunch (15–20)

Wednesday Row (15 Minutes)
Find any rowing machine

Alternate one-minute easy/one-minute hard

Thursday Lift (20 Minutes)

Barbell Bench Press
Pull-ups
Dumbbell Squat into Military Press

Friday Stretch (20 Minutes)

YouTube has thousands of videos; Pamela Reif is a personal favorite.

Saturday Lift (20 Minutes)

Barbell Power Clean and Press
Dumbbell Lunge with Bicep Curl
Push-ups with feet on Exercise Ball (15–20)

Sunday Walk (30–45 Minutes)

Walk off that cheat meal!

■ ■ ■

As Napoleon Hill once said, *"No person may enjoy outstanding success without good health."*

It should be no coincidence that many of the most successful people of our generation have discovered the undeniable connection between personal fitness and sustained success.

Whether you want to become a more influential leader, compound your prosperity, build a lasting legacy, or refine your craft, make sure a *healthy diet* and *physical exercise* are part of your daily routine.

LOVE . . . ACTUALLY?

"It's the Most Wonderful Time of the Year"

Those are the words that begin Andy Williams' famous 1963 song.

Regardless of what you celebrate, the holiday season is magical in many ways.

From decorating cookies with your children, to cuddling by the fireplace with your spouse, to opening presents with your family . . . the holiday season is truly memorable.

But what if you are single?

What if—rather than bake cookies with your kids—you find yourself eating raw Pillsbury Christmas Tree cookie dough straight from the box?

What if—rather than cuddle with your spouse—the only cuddling you're doing is with the throw blanket your ex purchased from *TJ Maxx*?

What if—rather than opening presents with family—you find yourself watching *The Christmas Story* marathon while drinking spiked eggnog?

While these examples are not personal in nature (ok . . . *maybe* the TJ Maxx blanket), let's face it: *the holiday season can be tough on singles.*

If you know, you know.

■ ■ ■

"Oh gosh Jared—here you go again!" you may be thinking. *"Why should I care about relationships?"*

While you may be happily married, remember that 50% of American adults have or will experience divorce at some point in their lifetime.[28] Furthermore, it is estimated that 30% of American adults are single at any given point in time . . . meaning that many readers—or many of the employees you supervise— share my perspective.

In 2021 I experienced my first "single" holiday season in 8 years. Although not an eternity, I was used to sharing the holidays with my (now ex) wife. And while spending time with family and friends was enjoyable . . . I found it difficult to fully embrace the "holiday spirit."

For example, let's discuss Christmas trees. In the past, putting up the Christmas tree was highly anticipated as it marked the beginning of the holiday season. In our house, it was common to blast some holiday tunes, crack open a bottle of Moscato d'Asti, and share some laughs while decorating O *Tannenbaum*. And while my contributions were often minimal, these nights produced some great memories.

This particular year, things were much different. Whereas many people quickly put up their tree after Thanksgiving, I postponed the event as long as possible. It wasn't until mid-December when I decided I should probably do something . . . only to realize that my ex took every holiday decoration we owned other than a mini-Christmas tree (which I proudly displayed in the living room).

Next, let's discuss commercials. As a kid, I always enjoyed watching advertisements on television during the holiday season. Whether it was Anheuser-Busch with their famous Clydesdales prancing through the snow, De Beers with their "A Diamond is Forever" holiday ad (search for "Palladio" and thank me later), or Corona with a single lighted palm tree in the Caribbean . . . there was always something memorable about holiday commercials.

This particular year, the holiday commercials hit different. No, VRBO—I don't want a private cabin getaway for my family of eight. No, Lindt Master Chocolatier with your fancy white hat,

I have no need for your holiday truffles. No, local Lexus dealership, I am not interested in your December to Remember sales event.

Finally, let's cover a topic to which all school leaders can relate: *the holiday potluck.* Potlucks are an honored school tradition, with the holiday version being the granddaddy of them all. The

The extent of my holiday decorating in 2021.

holiday potluck is a time for staff to celebrate the end of first semester while grazing on an endless smorgasbord of homemade dishes, dips, and desserts.

During potlucks, holiday plans are a common topic of discussion. In the past, these conversations were pretty straightforward: *"My wife and I are going to visit each other's families and spend some time together."* But in 2021, I felt embarrassed by my answer. Whereas most employees spoke of making memories with a spouse and kids, I found myself saying, *"I'm going home to see my parents"* as if I were a homesick college kid.

Before I go any further, let me be clear that I am being *overly dramatic on my assessment of singleness.* As you're about to find out, things aren't really that bad if you stick to a few core principles and focus on staying positive.

However, we cannot underestimate the challenges the holidays present. One recent study indicated that 88% of Americans identify the holiday season as the *"most stressful time of the year."* [29] Add in the fact that educator stress levels have skyrocketed in the post-COVID era, and there is a good chance that the holiday season is difficult on you or your "single" employees.

■ ■ ■

Ok, take a deep breath.

There are ways to survive—and even *thrive*—while being single during the holidays. Although I'm admittedly still a work in progress, here are six ideas that have helped:

Routine: Breaking from routine is fairly common during the holiday season as most people savor the opportunity to sleep in late and lounge around the house. While on the surface being "lazy" sounds enjoyable, in reality I have found that downtime is when I'm most vulnerable to negative thoughts. Ironically, sticking to a schedule and keeping myself busy prevents me from having feelings of loneliness and regret.

Hobbies: The difference between my divorce in 2021 and previous breakups was that I had something to keep my focus—which was writing this book. Rather than wake up lonely each morning because there was no one to share a bed with, I woke up feeling excited about my writing. What is your passion area? Finding something that keeps you motivated will help you stay grounded during times of adversity.

Give: Giving presents and making donations are scientifically proven to be good for your mental health. And what better time to give than during the holiday season? When I found myself single during the 2021 holidays, I committed to giving more than ever before. One of the most rewarding things I did was give away $1,500 worth of gift cards from local businesses to employees, students, and families.

Social Media: I have a love/hate relationship with social media. As a school leader and content creator, social media is part of my job. However, spending too much time on social media is a recipe for disaster! Not only do I become envious of other people's lives, I am also tempted to see what my ex is up to. My advice: *Stay away from social media during moments of vulnerability.* And when you do have to post something for work . . . get in and get out as quickly as possible!

Embrace the Funk: Regardless of who you are, we *all* go through funks. When this happens, realize you are in good company and tell yourself the following: *Feeling joy is impossible without also feeling the funk.* Down times should be viewed as learning opportunities. *How can I grow from this experience? What mistakes will I avoid in the future?* Remember—the funk will eventually end. And when it does, you'll be stronger as a result.

Focus on Yourself: Being single has some major advantages, and few are better than having *extra time* to improve yourself. What areas in your life do you want to upgrade? Apply for a new job. Invest more money. Take your dream vacation. Sign up for fitness classes. Start a side hustle. Many people realize that their full potential was being limited by a former partner.

■ ■ ■

Speaking of being limited by a partner, let's talk about *settling.*

My job has allowed me to meet hundreds of educators. And while most employees appear to be happy with their homelife, I can't help but notice a small percentage of staff who are adversely affected by their romantic relationships.

For many adults there is this idea that being with someone—*anyone*—is better than being alone. And while at times I have been guilty of having those same feelings . . . I have discovered that some employees are in really, *really* bad situations. When I hear their stories, I can't help but think, *"Why do they put up with that!?"*

One of my favorite books about relationships is *Relationship Goals* by Michael Todd. In his book, Todd discusses the misconception that you can't be happy unless you are with someone:

If you're single, I'm sure many people have made you feel like you aren't enough without a significant other. The pressure to find a mate seems intense and unyielding, and being single can start to feel shameful. Your life seems incomplete or even like a failure. This kind of thinking can cloud your judgment until you find yourself rushing into relationships that don't suit you, settling on someone—anyone—just to satisfy others and calm your fears.[30]

Consider your current situation.

Are you truly happy?
Or, are you settling?

For anyone who has read my previous work, you understand that I am a big proponent of refusing to settle in *any* aspect of life. Whether it be our jobs, our hobbies, our minds, or our relationships . . . we have limitless potential.

"But, Jared," you may be thinking. *"We've been together for soooo long! And we have soooo much history together!"*

In psychology, this is called the *sunk cost fallacy.* The sunk cost fallacy describes our natural bias to continue investing in something that is no longer serving us or might even be detrimental to us because of the time, cost, and effort we have invested.

Couples who are in bad or even toxic relationships will often stay because they feel like if they walk away, they will throw away everything they invested in the relationship. But rather than examine the past, people must consider the future.

Will I be happy with this decision 20 years from now?
Or, will I regret the relationship choices I made?

I'm not suggesting that we throw in the towel at the first signs of trouble. Couples should do what they can to salvage relationships, *especially* when kids are involved.

But when you're still miserable after years of trying to make things work, sometimes it's better to cut your losses. While ending relationships are never easy, understand that—in the long run—you could be much, *much* happier.

■ ■ ■

The last thing I want to do is pretend to be a relationship expert. My track record indicates I have a *lot* to learn.

However, as school leaders we must understand the dynamics of relationships. Specifically, we must learn how to empathize with staff.

When the holiday season arrives, don't assume that it's *"the most wonderful time of the year"* for all employees. In fact—for some of your staff—the holidays could be the most *difficult* time of the year.

HIGHLIGHTS AND LOWLIGHTS

While growing up, my mom had a tradition where she asked my siblings and I to share our "highlights and lowlights" during dinner. One by one, we shared the best part of our day (highlights) and the worst part of our day (lowlights).

At first, we loved sharing our moments, to the point where we argued over who got to go first. However, as the years went on, we got a little too "cool" for her games and developed elaborate excuses to avoid participating (*"If I don't share tonight . . . I'll share TWO highlights and lowlights tomorrow night!"*)

My mom—who was quite the clever woman—caught on to our tricks. Eventually, she instituted a rule which read: *"No one will leave the dinner table until everyone has shared their highlights and lowlights."* Although the term "mic drop" was not in vogue in the early 1990s, it was clear my mom was not messing around.

Now that I am older, I understand why my mom had us partake in this activity. Not only did it force us to talk to one another . . . it also gave us an opportunity to learn from our experiences. Slowly but surely, we learned to create more "highlights" while avoiding previous "lowlights."

Don't let the smiles and the silk shirts from K-Mart fool you, us Smith children were a rowdy bunch.

I now realize the importance of reflecting on the "highlights and lowlights" of our lives. One of my most productive habits is journaling what I've learned from my experiences—especially those experiences that don't go so well. Too often, we go through a bad situation and say, *"Well that sucked!"* but never take the time to pinpoint where things went wrong. By documenting the experience, the goal is to avoid similar mistakes in the future.

Another reflective practice I enjoy is to complete an annual review where I outline the most important things I learned over the past year. In early January, I spend time reviewing the biggest turning points of the past 365 days, and then describe how my mindset was changed. Similar to daily journaling, this process subconsciously helps me continue doing the "good stuff" while avoiding the "bad stuff."

As you can see, this process is not really about looking back . . . it's about *looking forward.* Completing an annual review forces me to look at my actions and ask, *"Are my choices helping me live the life I want to live?"*

■ ■ ■

To give readers an idea of what the process could look like, the following is the annual review I wrote for 2021:

Encourage Employee Feedback: In early 2021, our Director of Curriculum and I set a goal to meet with every district employee to ask for honest feedback on the district. This resulted in meeting with more than 250 employees across nearly 30 focus groups over a 2-month span. This process was highly beneficial because in addition to receiving valuable feedback, employees felt like their voices were being heard. These successful focus groups were the impetus behind arranging individual "rounding meetings" with certified employees. Rounding meetings quickly became a favorite professional practice, and will continue for years to come.

Our bus drivers were one of our most engaged focus groups!

Become a Better Listener: Early in my career, I heard that leadership was about asking questions. At the time, that concept didn't make sense: *"I thought leaders were supposed to tell people what to do?"* However, in 2021 I finally saw the light and realized that asking questions is a highly effective leadership practice. Now, when faced with a difficult decision, I immediately think, *"What questions do I need to ask the people who will be impacted by this decision?"* Staff who are asked to share their opinion feel like a part of process and are more likely to buy-in to a solution. Over the past year, I made more collaborative decisions—and less isolated decisions—than ever before in my leadership career.

Don't Take Things Personally: Let's be honest: *Most leaders are used to getting their way.* So, when others don't agree with an idea or push back on their thinking . . . leaders take things personally. For years, I struggled when others disagreed with my thinking and would dwell on the incident for hours. *"Who do they think they are?!"* I would seethe while lying in bed at night. However, this past year I stopped taking things so personally. I realized that in the big scheme of things, most decisions are fairly insignificant. Rather than assume I had to produce all of the ideas, my goal was to create a safe space where diverse opinions were shared. Saying phrases like, *"Feel free to push back on my thinking,"* and *"There are no right or wrong answers,"* became more common in conversations with employees.

> When faced with difficult decisions, leaders must think, *"What questions need to be asked of the people who will be impacted by this decision?"*
>
> **#TurningPoints**

 Smith, Jared <jsmith@s-tama.k12.ia.us>   Wed, Sep 9, 2020, 9:11 AM ☆ ↩ ⋮
to Chelsea, Anthony, Scott, Steve, Stephanie, Mark ▾

Good Morning Everyone!
This morning I was reminded of a website/company I texted a few of your about over the summer. The website is BoxOut Sports and the website can be found here. I was introduced to this company by a buddy of mine who is a coach and raves about the product and the social media graphics that can be created.

Here are links to examples of their work:

- BoxOut Sports on IG
- BoxOut Sports on Twitter
- BoxOut Sports on Facebook

Starting off at $480 for the year, I believe this could be a good investment and really give our graphics a clean, student-friendly look. Furthermore, I have a feeling this could go beyond athletics to be used in other areas.

However, I also realize I would not be the individual using the product, and therefore am simply going to throw this out there and "see what sticks." It won't hurt my feelings if you say no :)

When you have a few minutes feel free to share your thoughts. No rush!

Telling employees: "It won't hurt my feelings if you say no"
helps remove emotion from decisions.

Ignorance is Bliss: Over time, I have learned to stop worrying so much about things *outside* my control and instead focus on things *within* my control. Arguably, 2021 was a huge turning point for me in this regard. The first area was politics. While I have never cared much for politics, I gave *zero* attention to politics in 2021. I didn't look at the newspaper, I didn't read political posts, and I didn't watch the news. *"But Jared, don't you care about the world?"* Of course I want our world to be a better place, but I have discovered that politics does nothing but increase my anxiety and drain my energy. Another example—surprisingly—is sports. In the past, sports consumed my life. My happiness during a fall weekend literally depended on whether or not my football teams were winning. Whereas some people can watch sports just for fun, I can't help but fixate on the game which limits my ability to focus on anything else. When my teams were losing, I was no fun to be around! Eliminating politics and limiting sports resulted in a much more productive—and happier—year in 2021.

Pay it Forward: A few years ago, I created the "The 3% Rule" (see page 78) which contends when educators accept an administrative position, they must assume that 3% of their salary will go back to the school or district. In 2021, I fully embraced this concept by giving back to schools, employees, and the community more than ever before. While I wasn't raised in poverty, my siblings and I were on "free lunch" status for most of our lives. This frugal lifestyle taught me to be humble, responsible, and to do more with less. It also taught me to empathize with others and donate whenever possible. Now that I am in a financial position to give back to my community, I have adopted a giving mentality.

Positive Energy in Every Interaction: When people meet me, they assume I'm a positive and confident guy all the time. What they don't realize is that I'm a natural worrier, and my self-confidence runs hot and cold. To help improve this aspect of my life, I read a lot about interpersonal relationships over the past year. One of the best concepts I picked up was: *"Assume attraction until proven otherwise."* While originally meant to be dating advice, I have found that this wisdom can apply to *every* interaction. When meeting new people, I tend to worry too much about whether or not they "like" me as opposed to just being myself. Now, my goal is to approach every interaction with confidence. While still a work in progress, I have already noticed positive results.

Don't Worry, Be Thankful: My divorce was finalized in early 2021. Even though the ending of our relationship was my idea, I still battled constant feelings of regret and disappointment. Sick of the recurring negative emotions, I decided to journal about all of the things I was grateful for in our seven-year relationship. While there was plenty to be frustrated about . . . I also realized there was plenty to be thankful for. *"Wow . . . I wouldn't be who I am today had I never met Lindsey,"* I quickly realized. Rewiring my brain to look for the positives in difficult situations—whether it be a problematic coworker, a nagging injury, an untimely expense—was a huge turning point in my personal development.

Healthy Habits: How could I reflect on 2021 without mentioning the COVID pandemic? This year I was fortunate to maintain optimal health while others experienced severe health complications. I share this not to brag, but rather to support the notion that healthy habits are vital for living life to the fullest. I am convinced that those who are disciplined around working out, eating right, and prioritizing rest rarely struggle with COVID and the other health issues (heart disease, diabetes, etc.) of our time. I haven't missed a day of work due to illness in several years, and I credit my healthy habits as the reason why.

■ ■ ■

My mom still asks us to play "highlights and lowlights" when gathering for family meals.

While this request may garner the occasional eye roll from us kids, there is little doubt that this "game" has played a significant role in my approach toward life.

Recommended Reading:
Personal Growth

In addition to the books already referenced in *Turning Points*, below are fifteen more *personal growth* titles to add to your reading list. While not exhaustive, these resources provide a good starting point for anyone wanting to dig deeper into the "self-help" philosophies shared in these pages.

Books are arranged alphabetically by author.

- *Quiet*, by Susan Cain

- *Tribe of Mentors*, by Tim Ferriss

- *Relentless*, by Jim Grover

- *The Compound Effect*, by Darren Hardy

- *Everyday Millionaires*, by Chris Hogan

- *Didn't See That Coming*, by Rachel Hollis

- *Steal Like an Artist*, by Austin Kleon

- *Bird by Bird*, by Anne Lamott

- *Successful Aging*, by Daniel Levitin

‣ *Own the Day, Own Your Life,* by Aubrey Marcus

‣ *7 Strategies for Wealth & Happiness,* by Jim Rohn

‣ *The 5AM Club,* by Robin Sharma

‣ *Not a Diet Book,* by James Smith

‣ *Sleep Smarter,* by Shawn Stevenson

‣ *Crushing It!* by Gary Vaynerchuk

For more book ideas, visit *www.drjaredsmith.com/book-summaries*

CONCLUSION

"A journey of a thousand miles begins with a single step."[1]

—FROM *Tao Te Ching*
BY LAO TZU

Let me ask you: *How does it end?*

You can close these pages and say, *"That was good, I'll have to remember this stuff,"* as you place this book back on the shelf and return to everyday life much the same as it was before.

Or, you can close these pages and say, *"That was good, let's put these ideas into action,"* as you implement your favorite ideas for the purpose of making life better than it was before.

My hope is you embrace the lifelong learning lifestyle. Read books, journal about experiences, listen to podcasts, and learn from mentors. When you come across a golden nugget of truth or a quote that changes your perspective, file it away for future use.

In one year, you'll see progress as your influence becomes greater.
In five years, you'll notice a separation from your peers.
And in ten years, you'll be seen as an expert in your field.

Personal development is simple, but not easy.

Once you start to feel the positive, transformative impact of lifelong learning, your mindset will never be the same.

Looking For More?

If you've finished *Turning Points: More Lessons Learned on Leadership, Education, and Personal Growth* and are hungry for more, visit my website *www.drjaredsmith.com*. When you get there, check out the following:

Newsletter (drjaredsmith.com/newsletter): My newsletter offers bite-sized pieces of content on leadership, education, and personal growth each week. My goal is not to spam your inbox, but rather to share useful ideas to benefit your life.

Blog (https://www.drjaredsmith.com/articles): If you enjoyed the content shared in these pages, you'll want to check out my full list of blog entries. Each article provides practical insight, advice, and encouragement connected to everyday, real-life experiences.

Speaking (drjaredsmith.com/speaking): Seeing others improve as a result of what they are taught is highly motivating and brings me great pleasure. I would be honored to educate your audience on any of the principles covered in this book. Visit my website or email me at *dr.jaredrsmith@gmail.com*.

Podcast (drjaredsmith.com/podcast): The Group Project Podcast shares inspiring interviews from a wide-ranging group of successful individuals—perfect for anyone looking to enhance their professional and personal lives.

Book Summaries (drjaredsmith.com/book-summaries): If you enjoy getting book recommendations, you'll want to check my book summaries collection. I provide three big takeaways and other key ideas on hundreds of books on leadership, education, and personal growth.

About the Author

Dr. Jared Smith is the Superintendent of the Waterloo (Iowa) Community School District. With more than 10,000 students and 1,700 employees, Waterloo is among the 10 largest school districts in Iowa.

Jared has taught and coached at both the middle school and high school levels. Prior to becoming a superintendent, Jared worked as an assistant principal and principal for ten years.

Jared holds a BA in Elementary and Middle Level Education from the University of Northern Iowa, an MS in Educational Leadership from National Louis University, and a PhD in Educational Leadership from Iowa State University.

Jared is an award-winning blogger, professional speaker, and author of *Learning Curve: Lessons Learned on Leadership, Education, and Personal Growth.*

Thank You

To My Family: For always being my biggest fans and loving me unconditionally.

To My Friends: For giving me honest feedback on the pieces of this book that worked . . . and the pieces of this book that did not.

To the South Tama County and Waterloo Community School Boards: For your ongoing support of this book and the work you do for students.

To the South Tama County and Waterloo Community School Employees: For trusting me to share the ideas outlined in this book—many of which originated in your districts.

To My Blog Readers: For reading my work and providing feedback; your encouragement provided the motivation needed to complete this book.

To My Podcast Guests: For giving up your time to share your knowledge and passion; your ideas fueled much of what was written in this book.

To Vicki St. James: For being an amazing editor! For anyone needing a professional editor at an affordable price, visit *www .stjamesediting.com* or email her at *vs485539@gmail.com.*

To Shauna Smith: For always challenging my thinking and giving me the confidence to keep going.

To 1106 Design: Michele DeFilippo, Ronda Rawlins, and the entire team did an amazing job transforming my manuscript into a living, breathing book. Looking to self-publish? I would highly recommend you check out *https://1106design.com/.*

Endnotes

This section provides a detailed list of citations used throughout the book. I trust that most readers will find this list to be sufficient.

However, I also realize that literature changes over time and the references may need updating. Furthermore, isolated mistakes may occur—either in attributing an idea to the wrong person or not giving credit to someone where it is due.

If you believe this is the case, please email me at *dr.jaredrsmith @gmail.com* so I can fix the issue as soon as possible.

INTRODUCTION

1. Lombardi, V. (1970). *Run to daylight!* Grosset & Dunlap.

2. *Advice from Steve Martin.* YouTube. (2015, August 15). Retrieved August 29, 2022, from https://www.youtube.com /watch?v=teAvv6jnuXY

LEADERSHIP

1. Brown, B. (2018). *Dare to lead: brave work, tough conversations, whole hearts.* New York: Random House.

2. Hsieh, T. (2013). *Delivering happiness.* Grand Central Publishing.

3. *Snappy study reveals holiday gifts directly impact employee reten-tion.* Business Wire. (2021, November 3). Retrieved May 24, 2022, from https://www.businesswire.com/news/home/20211103005416 /en/Snappy-Study-Reveals-Holiday-Gifts-Directly-Impact -Employee-Retention

4. Wiseman, L., and S. R. Covey (2017). *Multipliers: How the best leaders make everyone smarter.* HarperBusiness, an imprint of HarperCollinsPublishers.

5. Elzinga, D. (2021, August 16). *The biggest lie in HR: People quit bosses not companies.* Culture Amp. Retrieved May 24, 2022, from https://www.cultureamp.com/blog/biggest-lie-peo ple-quit-bosses#:~:text=Our%20data%20showed%20that%20 the,12%25%20and%2011%25%20respectively.

6. Collins, J. C. (2001). *Good to great.* Harper Business.

7. Hattie, J. (n.d.). *Hattie Effect Size List—256 influences related to achievement.* Visible Learning. Retrieved May 24, 2022, from https://visible-learning.org/hattie-ranking-influences -effect-sizes-learning-achievement/

8. Covey, S. R. (2005). *The 8th habit: From effectiveness to great-ness.* Free Press.

9. Horstman, M. (2016). *The effective manager.* Hoboken, New Jersey: Wiley.

10. Kouzes, J. and B. Posner (2017). *The leadership challenge: how to make extraordinary things happen in organizations.* Somerset: John Wiley & Sons, Incorporated.

11. Lashinsky, A. (2013). *Inside apple: How America's most admired-and secretive-company really works.* Grand Central Pub.

12. Stanier, B. M. (2016). *The coaching habit: Say less, ask more & change the way you lead forever.* Box of Crayons Press.

13. Larson, E. (2021, December 10). *New research: Diversity + inclusion = Better Decision Making at work.* Forbes. Retrieved May 24, 2022, from https://www.forbes.com/sites/eriklarson/2017/09/21/new-research-diversity-inclusion-better-decision-making-at-work/?sh=36f5e8be4cbf

14. Bradley, J. (n.d.). *Cisco IBSG Horizons.* Retrieved May 24, 2022, from https://www.cisco.com/c/dam/en_us/about/ac79/docs/re/DDC_IBSG-Horizons.pdf

15. Kislik, L. (2022, February 1). *What do newer generations of employees want, and can your business adjust?* Forbes. Retrieved May 24, 2022, from https://www.forbes.com/sites/lizkislik/2022/01/28/what-do-newer-generations-of-employees-want-and-can-your-business-adjust/?sh=573981d12ee0

16. Marotta, A. (2017). *The principal: surviving & thriving: 125 points of wisdom, practical tips, and relatable stories for all leaders.* Andrew Marotta LLC.

17. Luna, T., and L. A. Renninger (2015). *Surprise: Embrace the unpredictable, engineer the unexpected.* Perigee Trade.

18. Schwartz, B. (2016). *The paradox of choice: Why more is less.* Ecco, an imprint of HarperCollins Publishers.

19. Levin, S. (2019, March 19). *Understanding and addressing principal turnover: A review of the research.* Learning Policy Institute. Retrieved May 24, 2022, from https://learningpolicyinstitute.org/product/nassp-understanding-addressing-principal-turnover-review-research-report#:~:text=The%20national%20average%20tenure%20of,for%2010%20years%20or%20more

20. Ferriss, T. (2017, June 14). *Esther Perel interview | the tim ferriss show (podcast)*. YouTube. Retrieved May 24, 2022, from https://www.youtube.com/watch?v=Hu-sCM0eXaw

21. Ahmed, A. (2021, March 15). *Report: 97 percent of gen Z consumers use social media platforms as their main source of shopping inspiration*. Digital Information World. Retrieved May 24, 2022, from https://www.digitalinformationworld.com/2021/03/report-97-percent-of-gen-z-consumers.html#:~:text=Report%3A%2097%20Percent%20of%20Gen,shopping%20inspiration%20%2F%20Digital%20Information%20World

22. Butler, D. (2021). *Permission to be great: increasing engagement in your school*. ConnectEDD.

23. Warren, E., and A. W. Tyagi (2006). *All your worth: The ultimate lifetime money plan*. Free Press.

24. Ramsey, D. (2013). *The total money makeover: A proven plan for financial fitness*. Nelson Books.

25. Dunn, E., and M. I. Norton (2014). *Happy money: The new science of smarter spending*. Simon & Schuster.

26. *Address of president-elect John F. Kennedy delivered to a joint convention of the General Court of the Commonwealth of Massachusetts, January 9, 1961*. (n.d.). Retrieved July 19, 2022, from https://www.jfklibrary.org/archives/other-resources/john-f-kennedy-speeches/massachusetts-general-court-19610109

EDUCATION

1. Sutcher, L. (2016, September). *A coming crisis in teaching?—learning policy institute*. Retrieved June 7, 2022, from https://learningpolicyinstitute.org/sites/default/files/product-files/A_Coming_Crisis_in_Teaching_REPORT.pdf

2. Glover, M. (2022, March 30). *Word of mouth marketing in 2022: Effective strategies + examples.* The BigCommerce Blog. Retrieved June 7, 2022, from https://www.bigcommerce.com/blog /word-of-mouth-marketing/#what-is-word-of-mouth-marketing

3. Peek, S. (2020, March 17). *Why employees quit (and how to reduce turnover rates).* business.com. Retrieved June 7, 2022, from https://www.business.com/articles/reasons-employees-quit/

4. Clifton, J., and J. K. Harter (2020). *It's the manager: Moving from Boss to coach.* Gallup Press.

5. Chapman, G. (2015). *The 5 love languages: The secret to love that lasts.* Northfield Publishing.

6. Chapman, G. D., and P. E. White (2019). *The 5 languages of appreciation in the workplace: Empowering organizations by encouraging people.* Northfield Publishing.

7. Heath, C., and D. Heath (2017). *The power of moments: Why certain experiences have extraordinary impact.* Simon and Schuster.

8. Whitaker, T. (2015). *What great principals do differently: Eighteen things that matter most.* Routledge.

9. Lencioni, P. (2012). *The advantage.* Jossey-Bass.

10. Murphy, D., and M. B. Ginsberg (2002, May 1). *How walkthroughs open doors.* ASCD. Retrieved June 7, 2022, from https ://www.ascd.org/el/articles/how-walkthroughs-open-doors

11. Goldring, E. (2015). *Making Time for Instructional Leadership* [Scholarly project]. Retrieved from https://www.wallacefoundation .org/knowledgecenter/Documents/Making-Time-for-Instructional -Leadership-Vol-3.pdf

12. Steinbach, R. (n.d.). *Employees want feedback—but no one is giving it.* Recruiter.com. Retrieved June 28, 2022, from https ://www.recruiter.com/recruiting/employees-want-feedback-but-no -one-is-giving-it/#:~:text=The%20problem%20is%2C%20 employees%20aren,feedback%20than%20they%20currently%20get

13. Zenger, J., and J. Folkman (2017, June 27). *The ideal praise-to-criticism ratio.* Harvard Business Review. Retrieved June 28, 2022, from https://hbr.org/2013/03/the-ideal-praise-to-criticism

14. Benner, M. (2020, July 8). *One size does not fit all.* Center for American Progress. Retrieved June 28, 2022, from https://www .americanprogress.org/article/one-size-not-fit/

15. Henderson, A.T., and K.L. Mapp. 2002. *A New Wave of Evidence: The Impact of School, Family, and Community Connections on Student Achievement.* National Center for Family and Community Connections with Schools, Southwest Educational Development Laboratory.

16. J. Casas, (2017). Culturize: every student, every day, whatever it takes. San Diego, California: Dave Burgess Consulting, Incorporated.

17. Gigande, E. (2021, November 4). *OSHA releases emergency temporary standard requiring mandatory vaccination or weekly testing for employers with 100 or more employees.* Law and the Workplace. Retrieved June 28, 2022, from https://www .lawandtheworkplace.com/2021/11/osha-releases-emergency -temporary-standard-requiring-mandatory-vaccination-or-weekly -testing-for-employers-with-100-or-more-employees/

18. Drucker, P. (2011). *The Effective Executive: The Definitive Guide to getting the right things done.* HarperCollins US.

19. Coe—Public School Expenditures. (2022, May). Retrieved June 28, 2022, from https://nces.ed.gov/programs/coe/indicator/cmb

20. Brooks, C. (2020, January 22). *Historically speaking: How lawsuits against schools are tying the hands of teachers.* The Morning Call. Retrieved June 28, 2022, from https://www.mcall.com/opinion/mc-opi-historically-speaking-six-brooks-20200123-kg zimsjzpfbnhnzvk2ewfu7mvi-story.html

21. Transactional Records Access Clearinghouse (TRAC)—comprehensive, independent, and nonpartisan information on federal enforcement, staffing and funding. (2017, August 16). Retrieved June 28, 2022, from https://trac.syr.edu/tracreports/civil/478/

22. Shrider, E. A. (2021, September 14). *Income and poverty in the United States: 2020.* Census.gov. Retrieved June 28, 2022, from https://www.census.gov/library/publications/2021/demo/p60-273.html#:~:text=Median%20household%20income%20was%20%2467%2C521,median%20household%20income%20since%202011

23. *Email marketing vs. SMS Marketing: You're asking the wrong question.* Campaign Monitor. (2022, March 3). Retrieved June 28, 2022, from https://www.campaignmonitor.com/blog/email-marketing/sms-marketing-vs-email-marketing/#:~:text=The%20facts%2C%20statistics%2C%20and%20the,to%20respond%20to%20an%20email

PERSONAL GROWTH

1. Sincero, J. (2017). *You are a badass: How to stop doubting your greatness and start living an awesome life.* Running Press.

2. Ben-Shahar, T. (2007). *Happier: Learn the secrets to daily joy and lasting fulfillment.* McGraw-Hill.

3. Gilbert, D. T. (2007). *Stumbling on happiness.* Vintage.

4. Jenkinson, C. E. (2013, August 23). *Is volunteering a public health intervention? A systematic review and meta-analysis of the health and survival of Volunteers—BMC Public Health.* Retrieved July 10, 2022, from https://bmcpublichealth.biomed central.com/articles/10.1186/1471-2458-13-773

5. Clear, J. (2018). *Atomic habits: An easy & proven way to build Good Habits & Break Bad Ones.* Avery, an imprint of Penguin Random House.

6. (DCD), D. C. D. (2021, October 20). *What are the five major types of anxiety disorders?* Retrieved July 19, 2022, from https ://www.hhs.gov/answers/mental-health-and-substance-abuse /what-are-the-five-major-types-of-anxiety-disorders/index.html

7. *Facts & Statistics: Anxiety and Depression Association of America, ADAA.* (n.d.). Retrieved July 19, 2022, from https ://adaa.org/understanding-anxiety/facts-statistics

8. *Jerry Seinfeld—A comedy legend's systems, routines, and methods for success | the tim ferriss show.* (2020, December 11). Retrieved July 19, 2022, from https://www.youtube.com /watch?v=yNTmFORn3xQ

9. Flannery, M. E. (2018, March 28). *The epidemic of anxiety among today's students.* Retrieved July 19, 2022, from https://www.nea.org/advocating-for-change/new-from-nea /epidemic-anxiety-among-todays-students

10. Allen, D. (2015). *Getting things done: The art of stress-free productivity.* Penguin Books.

11. Carroll, R. (2018). *The Bullet Journal Method: Track the past, order the present, design the future.* Portfolio/Penguin.

12. Kleon, A. (2019). *Keep going: 10 ways to stay creative.* Workman.

13. Hill, N. (2005). *Think and grow rich.* TarcherPerigee/Penguin.

14. Vermeeren, D. (2007, September 12). *Why people fail to achieve their goals.* Retrieved July 19, 2022, from https://www.reliableplant.com /Read/8259/fail-achieve-goals#:~:text=This%20is%20especially%20 prevalent%20among,they%20have%20set%20for%20themselves

15. Rohn, J. (2011). *The five major pieces to the life puzzle a guide to personal success.* Embassy Books.

16. Ingraham, C. (2021, November 24). *Analysis | leisure reading in the U.S. is at an all-time low.* Retrieved July 20, 2022, from https://www.washingtonpost.com/news/wonk/wp/2018/06/29 /leisure-reading-in-the-u-s-is-at-an-all-time-low/

17. Covey, S. R. (2014). *The 7 Habits of Highly Effective People: Powerful Lessons in Personal Change.* Simon & Schuster.

18. Grover, T. (2021). *Winning: The unforgiving race to greatness.* Scribner.

19. *The importance of self-discipline.* (2013, January 22). Retrieved July 20, 2022, from https://www.adventisthealthcare.com /living-well/the-importance-of-self-discipline/

20. Levitin, D. J. (2020). *Successful aging: A neuroscientist explores the power and potential of our lives.* Dutton.

21. Courrege, D. (2016, December 8). *Most teachers just wanna have lunch.* Retrieved August 20, 2022, from https://www .postandcourier.com/news/most-teachers-just-wanna-have-lunch /article_f42c6131-041a-5303-98b7-c83e838f9c64.html

22. Crowley, C., A. J. Hamilton and H. S. Lodge (2019). *Younger next year: Live strong, fit, sexy, and smart—until you're 80 and Beyond.* Workman Publishing.

23. *How to open a conversation with teens about healthy eating.* (2018, February 20). Retrieved August 20, 2022, from https://www.nationaleatingdisorders.org/blog/how-open -conversation-teens-about-healthy-eating

24. Petre, A. (2021, May 20). *Does calorie counting work? A critical look.* Retrieved August 20, 2022, from https://www.healthline .com/nutrition/does-calorie-counting-work#difficulty-losing -weight-when-counting-calories

25. Northwestern Medicine. (n.d.). *The Skinny on Cheat Days.* Retrieved August 20, 2022, from https://www.nm.org/healthbeat /healthy-tips/nutrition/the-skinny-on-cheat-days#:~:text =Research%20shows%20that%20after%20a,energy%20 balance%20in%20the%20body

26. Decathlon Blog. (2019, December 16). *11 benefits of Brisk Walking & How to start walking briskly.* Retrieved August 20, 2022, from https://blog.decathlon.in/articles/6-things-that -happen-to-your-body-if-you-do-a brisk- walk#:~:text=Brisk%20 walking%20can%20help%20you,increases %20your%20lean%20 muscle%20mass.&text=This%20method%20gets%20you%20 in,lose%20the%20calories%20you%20consumed

27. Matthews, M. (2018). *Bigger leaner stronger: The simple science of building the ultimate male body.* Oculus.

28. *Marriage and divorce.* (n.d.). Retrieved August 20, 2022, from https:// www.apa.org/topics/divorce-child-custody#:~:text=Marriage %20%26%20 divorce&text=They%20are%20also%20good%20 for,subsequent%20marriages%20is%20even%20higher

29. Anderer, J. (2022, May 17). *Jingle Bell Crock: 88% of Americans feel the holiday season is most stressful time of Year.* Retrieved August 20, 2022, from https://www.studyfinds.org/jingle-bell

-crock-88-of-americans-feel-the-holiday-season-is-most-stressful
-time-of-year/

30. Todd, M. (2020). *Relationship goals: How to win at dating, marriage, and sex.* Crown Publishing Group, The.

CONCLUSION

1. Tzu, L. (1997). *Tao Te Ching.* CreateSpace.

Made in the USA
Middletown, DE
29 November 2022

16345403R00179